SUBUD
A SPIRITUAL JOURNEY

Some Unsought Encounters on the Way

By Rozak Tatebe

Copyright © 2008 Rozak Tatebe
All rights reserved.

ISBN: 1-4196-9184-8
ISBN-13: 9781419691843

Library of Congress Control Number: 2008901695

Visit www.booksurge.com to order additional copies.

"Subud" is the registered mark of the "World Subud Association".

The views and beliefs presented in this book are exclusively those of the author and can not be construed as being those of the World Subud Association.

I would like to express my heartfelt thanks to Savana Simpson and Ilaina Lennard who made it possible for me to publish this book. Savana translated my Japanese manuscript into English, and Ilaina proofread the text for me, and made editorial revisions to it.
(17th November 2007)

CONTENTS

In Search of Direct Contact with the Supreme Being

PROLOGUE	3
The Fire of the Creator	5
The Soul, what is it?	8
Two Experiences	11
Childhood Environment	14
The Search	22
A Significant Encounter	30
The Latihan of Subud	37
Misunderstanding and Confusion	41
The Trials Begin	44
Trials and Rescue	49
Early Spiritual Experiences	59
The Ultimate Inner Experience	67
Sumiko	70

Pillar of Light	93
The Supreme Goal	100
The arrow that pierced my heart	101
Bapak's Spirituality	113
The Inner Bapak	113
The Outer Bapak	118
Bapak's Mission	128
Tests by Bapak	135
Testing and the Outer Life	146
Religion and the Latihan	150
On Death	162
Death of a Friend	167
The Realm of Death	171
A Departure Worthy of Celebration	173
Sincere Receiving	177
The World Congress in Colombia	180
EPILOGUE	191

SECTION I

In Search of Direct Contact with the Supreme Being

PROLOGUE

This is not an autobiography.
It is the story of how, through a sudden,
extraordinary experience, I came to know the existence
of the Supreme Being, the Creator of the Universe.
Tasting that moment of true bliss, my undeveloped
soul sought to recover lost time and experience contact
with the Supreme Being.
This is a record of the unpredictable trials and
events that unfolded through my soul's chance
encounter with a spiritual training. Many of these
stories will appear outside the realm of common sense.
But everything that happened was real
And each incident has been recounted exactly
as it happened.

Fire of the Creator

The first thing I want to write about is an experience that led me to start my search for the Creator of the Universe, and which set my soul on the first step of its journey. This was an experience for which I was totally unprepared, that came to me suddenly and for which I have no ordinary explanation.

At the time, I was 21 and a university student. I was living in a small room in a two storey building in Tokyo that was like a student dormitory. One day, around noon, I was sitting idly on the tatami mat with nothing in particular to occupy me, when suddenly, it felt as though something around me had changed. In the next moment, I was confronted with a strange sight. I saw a sun which was burning with an incredible radiance – burning because of some Power that I have no words to describe. Perhaps one could call it the Fire of the Creator. The sun was burning because of this Fire. And what was remarkable was that even the earth, and even my inside was burning with that same Fire.

It was as though I could see right through to the core of the earth, and it was filled and burning with this Fire of the Creator. And spread in a thin layer around the surface of the earth was the ecosystem which covered it like a shell. And even though parts of it were dirty and discoloured and repulsively shrunken, it still all sparkled with that Fire.

'This is the Fire of God!' I thought to myself. I felt at that moment that I was looking at the Creator of the Universe.

What was even more surprising was that the moon was also filled with the same Fire. The cold, lifeless moon that until now I had thought was just a dead, silent lump of matter was now filled with the Fire of the Creator and was alive and sparkling. I found myself staring in amazement at the incredible sight of the sun, the moon, and the earth all filled with this Fire.

Then, aware that none of the other celestial bodies had entered my consciousness, I turned my attention to them. As an experiment, I focused my attention on Mars. And as I did so, I could see that Mars too was filled with the Fire of the Creator. But I could only feel its existence as an incredibly distant, tiny dot.

Then, I turned my attention to the fixed stars outside the solar system. I couldn't remember any names then and there, so I thought about the star closest to our solar system, but all I could see was a something so faint that it was barely there. I was a little disappointed because it seemed to show that this was the limited extent of my consciousness.

I cannot remember how long I stayed gazing at this sight. It felt like it was a long time, but I'm sure in reality it was no more than one or two minutes. Gradually it began to diminish and when I came to, I was back sitting on the tatami mat. I looked around me, trying to sense that Fire in the walls or the columns around me. Maybe it was my imagination but I was still aware of the faint trace of something until gradually that too dissipated.

This experience was entirely unexpected and unsought and it had an immeasurable impact on me. What I had seen was too real for me to doubt. It was as though I had witnessed proof of the existence of the Supreme Being, ruler of the universe – something that I had doubted until then. And that conviction was so strong that fundamentally it never changed, regardless of what situations I was to find myself in throughout the rest of my life from then on.

When I took my dishes to the sink, for some reason, I just started washing them - maybe it was because I felt bad that I had been so late. There were still dishes in the sink from people who had finished eating before me, and so I just started to wash those dishes too. And it was in that instant that again I suddenly felt the presence of the universe; I felt my connection to it. It is hard to describe but it felt as though the universe was like a soft, elastic continuum, and I was connected to it through the water tap. As I washed the dishes, it felt as if that act of washing someone else's dishes set up a vibration within the elastic continuum, like ripples on the surface of a lake, that seemed to reach to the very end of the universe. For me this was an entirely new sensation and what seemed to me like an important discovery: that even the most trivial act, the simplest thought, causes ripples in the universe that spread throughout its entirety and by doing so has some sort of effect on it.

The realisation did not end there and later, it became clear that it had brought about surprising changes in me. Because these changes were so undeniable, they proved to me that this experience had been more than simply a daydream.

The Soul, what is it?

These days, 'soul' is an ambiguous word. It is often used figuratively to signify different things - such as simply the heart's responses or a person's core belief. That is because people have already ceased to believe in a soul that really does exist within them. This is because science identifies humans as no more than physical entities, it negates the existence of anything beyond these.

But to deny a higher existence within humans is also to deny them the possibility to use this to link with the Power of the Supreme Being. People have ignored and eventually forgotten the potential for us to transcend this world and contact a spiritual realm that is under the direct control of the Power of that Supreme Being.

The common understanding of 'soul,' if it is not to do with ghosts, is that it is something present deep within one's being. And it is suggested that a 'spiritual experience' - if it is not to be at most, the 'transcendence' that Abraham Maslow refers to as feelings of inexplicable happiness or rapture - should be regarded as psychic or supernormal phenomenon, regardless of whether one believes in them or not.

However, in spite of how mysterious they may appear, most of these supernatural events occur in a dimension that is still within reach of the human mind. Humans can still intervene or manipulate them.

A true spiritual experience however, transcends the realms of the mind. It is born of an encounter between the soul, and the Sacred Power. It is an experience granted from above. It cannot be obtained through desire or effort.

SUBUD – A SPIRITUAL JOURNEY

However, in modern society, ruled as it is by secular knowledge and consciousness, the blessings of such an experience appear unattainable. Gurus market supernatural powers to win people over. It seems that such leaders are not fully aware of the potential given to human beings to actually experience something that transcends material profits and values. But that experience is at work like a subterranean stream, building the invisible bridge between the Creator and humankind.

The experiences that I will talk about in this book are all within the scope of my own limitations, and therefore may suffer from being too individual. But they may also stand as one man's testimony to the reality of this bridge between the Creator and humankind.

Now, as to the change I had within myself as the result of my first experience, it had something to do with the idea of Karma. The idea that as you sow so shall you reap, has been widely accepted for a long time in many religions; heaven eventually rewards you if you stack up your virtuous deeds without advertising them. At the time, I was so convinced of this that I secretly expected I would get some reward for even the most trivial deed. Whenever I did anything I deemed virtuous, the thought of reward would cross my mind. The idea occupied my mind more and more, and I just couldn't get rid of it.

Once, when I caught myself anticipating yet another brownie point from heaven after I had tidied away the shoes that were scattered around the front door, I shuddered in self-disgust. I wanted to free myself and longed to behave in a non-reward-orientated kind of way. But it was as if I were caught in a mental trap – the more I tried not to think about reward, the more the idea dogged me, and the more I struggled to free myself, the tighter the trap became.

And then, unexpectedly, I found myself completely free from the expectation of reward. Regardless of how I behaved, the idea no longer crossed my mind. Even when I deliberately turned my attention to the thought, it held no interest - as though it had no connection to me. This was startling, and a blessing that, because it happened with absolutely no effort, appeared nothing short of a miracle. I realised that for reasons I could not explain, I was now released from reward-based thinking so I could live my life with greater freedom.

Two Experiences

Needless to say, after my initial experience, I was filled with elation. The message I had received was that the Supreme Being was all happiness and joy, and that to know His existence was also to experience that happiness and joy. I wanted to tell others that truth. The elation lasted two or three months, and then gradually faded, but meanwhile, I had two other fairly strange experiences.

SUBUD – A SPIRITUAL JOURNEY

The first one was the experience of hearing the ultimate sound that I believe love produces. One day, I was lying on my bed, lost in a daydream, when suddenly, I heard a sound in the sky on my left, which seemed to be getting gradually closer and louder. But no sooner did I think it was right above me, than it suddenly veered off to the right, though it was still above me. The whole thing took just 4 to 5 seconds. What I heard was not a melody but one long continuous note – a note that was filled with a heavenly sweetness. It was strange but when I heard that intensely beautiful sound, my daydream vanished, and I felt completely refreshed. The thought that this was the sound that love itself does indeed produce, instantly flickered across my mind. It filled me with an unworldly euphoria.

Even to this day, I have no idea why I thought that this was the sound produced by love. There is nothing to prove that it was anything more than the sound of a passing aircraft. That love has a sound or that a sound can be love seems irrational. But to me, the truth is that it was different from any sound that exists on earth. I can only say that it had a heavenly resonance. It felt as though that sound had fallen by accident out of Heaven, and had hovered in the earth's atmosphere for a moment. I had been doubtful of the existence of such a dimension, but from that time, I started to consider the probability that it did exist after all.

At that time in Tokyo, trams were a convenient way for people to get around the city. Another unforgettable experience happened while I was riding in one of them. A few people were hanging onto the leather straps while the rest were seated; most were shabbily dressed with worn and harassed faces. There were apron-clad women with shopping bags, middle-aged men in work dress, old men and women in worn-out clothes nodding off to sleep. None of this was unusual, but for the fact that I could see quite clearly through the passengers' bodies to the beautiful, clear souls that glowed like crystal in the breast of each one of them. My impression was that they had souls as beautiful as the Bodhisattva of Compassion, (the Buddhist deity of Mercy). I could not believe what I was seeing. But even when I blinked my eyes, the scene in front of me remained unchanged.

Though it had only lasted a few seconds, I was left with a puzzling enigma. If what I had witnessed was real, how could it be that these people, whose souls were as beautiful as the Bodhisattva of Compassion, were unaware of it and lived wretched lives distanced from the beauty of their souls? And why should they have to live such miserable lives?

The answer was beyond me. Buddhism, Christianity, and most other religions teach that each person has a fragment of the Divine Spark or the Buddha nature within them. Perhaps this was what I had seen – but even if so, it still did not answer my question. No matter how I tried, I could not find an answer and the riddle remained a riddle.

I remained in this state of heightened consciousness for two to three months, during which time I had had these two parallel experiences. I was filled with the bliss of knowing the real existence of the Supreme Being called God, the Creator. But all experiences are temporal. It is because of this that even the most painful eventually settle at the bottom of our memories, allowing us to recover gradually from the anguish.

In particular, as the joy and elation that I had felt were so different from a state of excitement, whenever I tried to evoke my state again, all I could feel was an acute sense of loss. And that was what finally triggered my pursuit of God, the Creator.

But before I elaborate on this, let me provide more background to these early experiences and to my family environment.

Childhood Environment

Due to the nature of my father's work I was born in North Korea which was a Japanese colony before the war. When I was three, we moved to Seoul where we lived until the end of the war. My father and mother were dedicated followers of the spiritual movement of Seicho-no-Ie (Truth of Life), and from the moment I was able to reason, my upbringing was heavily influenced by this.

The trigger for my father joining Seicho-no-Ie was my mother's glaucoma. At that time glaucoma was an incurable illness. Even now, there is absolutely nothing that can be done except to slow the progress of the disease with drugs. All the doctors told my mother that she would go completely blind in a few years. Resigned to the fact, she started making preparations for her life after she had become blind. She took up the *shamisen* (traditional three-stringed instrument) so that she could have something to give her pleasure, and it became my custom to go to sleep listening to her plucking the strings of the instrument. Then one day, my mother heard Dr. Taniguchi, the founder of Seicho-no-Ie, talking about how we are all children of God, and that originally illness did not exist. This meant that one could cure it by changing the state of one's mind. She started to have some hope.

My parents both went to Tokyo to be close to the headquarters of Seicho-no-Ie and rented a room nearby. For more than a month, they attended Dr. Taniguchi's talks every day. They also worked hard to study the meditation practice of Seicho-no-Ie and read aloud the revelation that Dr. Taniguchi had received. My mother had several experiences during this time; one she often spoke about was how on a certain morning, when she set out, each leaf on the trees lining the road seemed to shine brilliantly as though the world had been completely transformed.

Then suddenly, she had a miraculous recovery from her glaucoma. After that, my mother and father offered their house as a base for the Korean branch of Seicho-no-Ie. They themselves became local teachers and worked devotedly to spread Dr. Taniguchi's teachings. Because she had had the personal experience of being cured of glaucoma – a supposedly incurable disease - my mother, in particular, was devoted to Dr. Taniguchi, and so absolute was her faith that more than a few people taught by her were able to conquer their own illnesses.

Besides illness, most of the problems people took to my mother were issues between couples or between parents and children. Many of these were out of the ordinary, such as parents with a son who was schizophrenic and violent, a mother whose daughter was possessed, and even a housewife who said she was capable of astral travel and could go wherever she pleased, but her bad hips prevented her from walking.

The parents of the schizophrenic youth were too afraid to even enter his room so my mother would go in and talk to him. He started to trust her as a mother, after which he often came to visit our house. He would arrive in the middle of winter when it was 10 degrees below zero, wearing only sandals on bare feet and a light bathrobe, smiling away and muttering to himself; stay a couple of hours, and then just take off back home. My mother told me he was intelligent and that I should ask him to help me with my maths. So then, I also got used to him and did not find him frightening. (He slowly improved and after the war, was able to marry and get a job.)

This was the situation with my mother while I was growing up. During that time I also had some experiences which were frightening for a child. Once, my mother had the girl who was possessed stay over at our house. It was summer and my mother, the girl and I were all sleeping under one mosquito net with my mother in the middle. As my mother often had people stay over, and as she had not explained anything to me about our guest, I did not think there was anything unusual about her. But in the middle of the night, I was awoken by strange noises. My mother was in conversation with the girl. The spirit that had taken possession of her was proclaiming in a deep, masculine voice that he was the highest god of the universe. In response, my mother was telling him that he was no such thing and indeed no more than a lowly spirit. I stiffened as I heard this, but as soon as I moved even slightly the girl shouted in a piercing voice, "here comes another one!"

Afterwards, my mother told me that the spirit who possessed the girl had told her that she would die if she were to eat, and so she had been refusing food. My mother, however, had persuaded her to eat something the next morning, and needless to say, nothing happened to her.

Science and medicine do not recognize healing through prayer and faith, but I was able to witness this actually happening around my mother. Of course, not all diseases were cured, but neither was it the case that all the illnesses that were cured by faith were due to misdiagnoses or quackery.

Beside these, I myself had one small experience concerning Seicho-no-Ie. This occurred when my mother first took me to a Seicho-no-Ie meeting. I was still very young and of course understood nothing as I sat beside her. Thirty minutes of the time was devoted to meditation, so I copied the adults, closed my eyes, put my hands together and sat on the floor with my legs under me. After about fifteen minutes, my legs got pins and needles and unable to bear it any longer, I stretched them out, opened my eyes, and looked around me. For no particular reason, I glanced at my left wrist. A few months earlier, a wart had formed there and it had gradually grown to quite some size. But when I glanced at the wart now, it had halved in size. No matter how much I looked, there was no mistaking the fact that it had shrunk. I hastened to shut my eyes again, refold my legs and put my hands together. After the final five minutes was up, I opened my eyes and cautiously cast another glance at my wart. But it had disappeared without trace, and my skin was completely smooth where the wart had been.

Maybe it often happens that warts disappear over time before you remember to look at them, but for a wart to disappear in only thirty minutes, and not only that but to have oneself also witnessed the disappearance halfway through, cannot be considered an ordinary occurrence. In fact there was something else that was puzzling. The person I had seen running the meeting was a middle-aged man of large build who had a black beard and was wearing traditional Japanese clothing. However, when I asked my mother about him on the way home, she said there had been no-one of that description there. I had seen that man during the meeting and so my mother's words did not make sense to me, but she assured me there was no-one like that amongst the followers of Seicho-no-Ie. The issue was never resolved.

That is how I was brought up; it was in an environment where faith-healing was pretty much a normal occurrence. By the time I was in junior high school, I had absorbed a religious knowledge and way of thinking through Dr. Taniguchi's writings, and began to learn about my own way of life. Dr. Taniguchi taught that all religions were based on the same truth, but that they were looked at from different angles. From this platform he expounded a philosophy and practice of idealism. To these he added his own analysis of Buddhism, Christianity, and Shinto doctrine, and used Christian Science and psychoanalysis to show that the world of truth was the real world, a world of ultimate perfection, and the phenomena of this world were just shadows of the mind.

Japan's defeat in the war shook my way of life to the core. Most religions in Japan were aligned with the belief that Japan was the land of the gods and they went along with the army's strategy of war. With the defeat, people's trust in religion fell away. As the old values shattered, Japan's society was transformed from being one that was predominantly spiritual to one that was largely material.

After we were repatriated back to Japan, I enrolled in a preparatory course for a newly established university and for three years lived in a dormitory in a suburb of Shimizu City. There, I lived with students of my own age in an entirely secular environment. As I discussed with them the left-wing ideas that dominated post-war society, I lost the naivety that I had grown up with, and became a sceptical youth with the pessimism of one who even carries around cyanide as a suicide pill.

However, something was to pour cold water on that death wish: a good friend from amongst my fellow students attempted suicide. He swallowed a large number of sleeping pills and then came into my room to say goodbye. As he talked, his speech started to sound strange and finally he confided to me that he was going to commit suicide. We had shared our weariness of life, and as we talked, I became extremely hesitant about whether I should allow him to die there and then. In the end, I could not allow it, and as he was already half asleep I called a lecturer and saved him. He reproached me bitterly when he came to, but he never tried to commit suicide again. Until then, he had adored Kirkegaard and would often quote his aphorism, "marry or do not marry, you will regret it either way," but he had a change of attitude and became instead a vehement communist. By saving him against my own beliefs, my own death wish had been nipped in the bud, and I was no longer able to contemplate suicide.

After my years of preparatory study, I enrolled in Tokyo University and that became a turning point in my life. I had previously forgotten all about the Seicho-no-Ie spiritual group, but fresh contact with them was now established. This was because while I had been boarding at a local dormitory, at the wish of Dr. Taniguchi my mother had relocated to Tokyo to work for Seicho-no-Ie and had become a teacher at their headquarters. As it was my first time in Tokyo and I had no friends there, at my mother's suggestion, I joined the youth section of Seicho-no-Ie so that I could make new friends.

Most of the members were like me, second generation members whose parents were followers of Dr. Taniguchi. Unlike me, they had maintained their faith since childhood. In fact, it would be truer to say that the youth section consisted entirely of young people like these. All of them - men and women alike, were cheerful, pleasant young people who often mentioned 'God' without a hint of doubt. But, the more I spent time with them, the more I myself started to feel uncomfortable with the word 'god'.

They continually repeated their god's name, but did they really accept 'its' existence, I wondered? I could not believe they did, but I hesitated to say so. If I had done, no doubt they would with considerable tolerance, have spent a lot of effort trying to convince me of 'its' existence.

What I was looking for was not theoretical proof. What I wanted was something else, that would absolutely convince me that God existed. The more honest I was with myself, the less I knew whether I actually did believe in 'Its' existence. The question began to weigh more heavily on me. I soon worked my way into an impasse.

The experience that I had of the Fire of the Creator - which I talked about at the beginning of this book, occurred while I was in this state.

The Search

In Zen, people talk about the extreme ecstasy experienced by one who achieves enlightenment, as one where "arms flutter and legs move spontaneously" - in other words, a state of such joy that the body starts to dance of its own accord. I had tasted a similar state after I had experienced the existence of the Supreme Being, but after two to three months, the feeling of bliss began to subside, and I felt I was returning to my former state. I was aghast at how different this was.

But there was no doubt I had changed after that experience – not only my way of thinking but to some extent, my personality had also changed. I now believed in 'God', I was no longer a cynical, frowning youth. Yet when I looked inside myself I knew that much of me was still the same. The weaknesses in my character had not changed, and my emotional responses were as before. I got offended at the slightest things – and this would then swing me back into a negative state.

I so longed to recapture the bliss that I had been given. I wanted to find a way to get hold of it again. I had tasted rapture and now I could not go on living without it. That was the beginning of my search.

I wanted to determine the nature of my experience and whether there had been similar cases to my own in the past. But unlike now, there were only a handful of books on religion or spirituality available in Japan. Finally, my efforts took me to a book written by William James, called *The Varieties of Religious Experience*.

According to James, what I had experienced was a 'sudden conversion'. James refers to many cases from past writings, and analyzed what they had in common. He explains a sudden conversion as being an experience whereby, without premonition, a person suddenly encounters a phenomenon that causes them to feel a 'sacred' presence. At that moment, that person, who until now never believed or was never interested in God, is instantly transformed into a believer.

James defined a sudden conversion as 'the phenomenon whereby the main weight of a person's individual energies and interest shifts to the spiritual arena'. He compared these results with those in which someone gradually starts to believe, and concluded that while the processes that lead people to believing may differ, essentially there was no difference in the results. James also discusses whether there was some divine grace or providence working behind a sudden conversion, but as a scholar he prudently avoided drawing any conclusions.

I decided that my own experience had been of the sudden conversion type. While most of the examples of 'sudden conversion' that James quoted had occurred within a Christian context, the core content had no connection to the doctrines of any specific religion, but was just the experience of coming into direct contact with something sacred. In fact, my experience had also had nothing to do with religion but was closer to a beatific vision or a cosmic consciousness. It also had the nature of being something that could relate to several doctrines or theories.

To me, it seemed that this sort of experience was like the magma that issues from a volcano at eruption. When a volcano erupts, lava spews forth but when it spills over, it is still liquid and does not yet have a solid shape. Because it has to flow all the way from the top of the volcano to the bottom, it hardens on the way into different shapes depending on nearby topographical features. On reading James, it seemed to me that the origin of religion was of a similar nature, because the starting point of many, if not all religions, is when someone has a primal experience that can be likened to a volcano erupting. That person interprets the experience according to his/her cultural background. The experience is then communicated to the people of that time in terms they can understand, and this then becomes a religion or creed.

This can explain the differences that emerged between religious creeds. In other words, even though the feeling of connection to a God or to a sacred Presence may have been the same, variations in creed or in where emphases were placed, emerged through differences in the personalities of the founders and the culture of their times. This idea also underpins the notion that regardless of the diversity of religions, there is usually one Supreme Being at the core. Perhaps what I had experienced, even though not so major, was at least similar.

This had partially answered my first question. The next question was did the potential exist to recreate this type of experience or something similar to it?

What I was looking for was not the many gods of polytheism but a direct contact with The God as creator of the universe. I wanted to know if this experience was available to ordinary people and if there had been examples in the past, what were the conditions that had enabled them to occur? The first clue came unexpectedly in a book that I already had in my possession. The book was Meister Eckhart's *The Book of Divine Consolation*. It had been given to me by a respected Dean from my university preparatory course, who was called Shinsaku Aihara. The book was the first translation from the original Middle High German into Japanese, of a collection of sermons by Eckhart. Just before I had graduated, Mr. Aihara had given it to me as a graduation gift. I had kept it with me but had not read it yet.

There was an obvious example of contact with God by ordinary people in the time of the Bible at the first Pentecost, when the Holy Spirit descended from Heaven on each of those who had gathered after the death of Jesus. In Christianity, God and the Son and the Holy Spirit are seen as one, and contact with the Holy Spirit therefore, also signified contact with God. However, this event occurred in the special circumstances of the death of Jesus Christ and I could find no relevance in it to my case.

SUBUD – A SPIRITUAL JOURNEY

Eckhart is said to have been the greatest mystic in mediaeval Germany; a renowned scholar without peer who is known for having been the first in Germany to deliver sermons in German rather than in Latin so that ordinary people could understand. However, after his death, most of his teachings were deemed to be heretical by the Vatican because they preached the potential for direct contact with God. His works were all gathered and burned. Only those that had their titles changed for secrecy's sake survived until today.

Eckhart says that people should not be satisfied with a God thought about by the mind, as once the thought disappears, so does God. Therefore, people should have a God that essentially transcends the thoughts of humans and all created things. He described the state of heart and mind that makes this possible, as one of *'Abgeschiedenheit'* (separatedness). This separatedness is a state whereby the heart and mind surrender completely to the 'will of God' – a state close to nothingness that can be achieved when outside of one's ego. He used the following metaphor to make this idea more understandable.

When one writes on a sheet of paper, if there is something already on it, no matter how beautiful those letters or images are, they are an obstacle to the writer, who would do better with a blank page. In the same way, if God is to write something, one's mind needs to present a blank surface. This emptiness, close to the nothingness, is what existed before God created all things. Eckhart wrote that a human being in such a state would automatically be filled with God's Essence, and would see Him in all things.

After I had read Eckhart, I came across similar ideas in the works of St. John of the Cross — one of Spain's most well-known mystics during the Renaissance flowering of religious reform. St. John considered that the end point of the monastic life was to achieve a state of purity and emptiness. If one achieved that state, one would be capable of receiving the direct influence of the Holy Spirit. But, as he warned, one first had to go through many stages and harsh trials to survive along the way.

Through these examples, I discovered that there actually had been people who experienced a direct contact with a Supreme Being. While this gave me hope, it also caused me to feel dejected. I understood that the key to such a contact was to purify the mind so that it was in a state of emptiness. However, this required extraordinary strength of will and an abstemious discipline that seemed unachievable for an ordinary person like me.

I have mentioned only Christian examples, but the goal of Buddhist discipline is also for the mind to achieve a state of emptiness close to nothingness (*mu*). Zazen and other modes of Buddhism are all means to achieve that end, as they were considered to be the path to separation from the cycle of rebirth, in order to reach Nirvana. And even if you devote yourself to intense training, you are not guaranteed achievement of that nothingness.

Another thing that caused me to hesitate was the danger of being possessed by discarnate entities. When I was a child I had witnessed the strange behaviour of the girl possessed by a spirit. Regardless of whether there was a medical or psychological explanation, I now knew there was a very real possibility of this happening. If people are careless or do not have a proper teacher, they may attract these spirits. Dr. Taniguchi mentioned this in his autobiography when he talked about the danger from supernatural entities that he experienced as a young person doing the spiritual practice from the Omoto Shinto sect. According to him, the meditation in Seicho-no-Ie was specifically designed to avoid that danger.

And so, as a result of all my searching, I realized that even if it were not impossible, there was only a very slim chance of recapturing the experience I yearned for. Considering the state of society, it seemed no method existed nowadays that could fulfill my desire.

After I graduated from university, I entered the publishing company called Kyobunsha. This company had been founded by Dr. Taniguchi, and was mainly as a means to publish his writings. While it was principally the publishing arm of Seicho-no-Ie, it had expanded in order to publish works other than Dr. Taniguchi's and was particularly involved in translating and publishing works of psychoanalysis by Freud, Jung, and others.

I chose to work in Kyobunsha because I was interested in editing and because my childhood familiarity with Seicho-no-

Ie would also make it an easy environment in which to work. Ever since I had been given that vision of the Creator's Fire, I had become more interested in religion and felt that I wanted to live in a religious environment. But I had no expectation that by being inside Seicho-no-Ie I would find a way to recapture my own special experience, or that the meditation practices of Seicho-no-Ie would help me in that way. My own experience had been completely unexpected and bore no relation to their practices, but nevertheless it was essentially compatible with what Dr. Taniguchi used to say.

I started my time by editing the magazine for youth. After two or three years, I became editor of the main magazine for all the members. As this was like a personal monthly journal for Dr. Taniguchi, my relationship with him intensified from then on.

As a young editor, what I always hoped for was that the Seicho-no-Ie movement would not become an established religion. Dr. Taniguchi had started his group as a movement for ideas, not as a religion. His original idea had been not to rely on the members' donations to finance the group's operations, but to establish Kyobunsha, the enterprise, as a means to publish his own works and to support Seicho-no-Ie with the profits.

This was an entirely new concept for a spiritual movement – a revolutionary experiment even. However, the impact of losing the war and the resulting social change threatened the financial base of the group which then opted for recognition instead, and embarked on establishing itself as an official religion. Dr. Taniguchi and others tried hard to prevent this but did not succeed. Soon, Seicho-no-Ie went down the path of many new-age religions who direct their efforts towards strengthening their financial base by expanding the membership. Seicho-no-Ie put all its efforts into building a large centre to attract more members, instead of expanding welfare facilities such as the orphanage that Dr. Taniguchi had established for war orphans. I gradually became uncomfortable with this. At the same time, the feeling of nostalgia for my original experience coupled with the reality - that I had no way of recapturing it, served to strengthen my sense of despair. That in turn began to affect my health and I started to feel apathetic and weak.

It was at that time that I first met with the Englishman, Husein Rofe.

A significant encounter

My encounter with Husein Rofe was to be a turning point in my life, though at the time I would never have guessed it. Husein Rofe was an Englishman of Syrian extract. He was in his early thirties and it was through him that I was first introduced to the spiritual movement known as Subud.

My encounter with him was the result of several overlapping coincidences.

One morning in 1954, a minor issue arose in the editing department of the Kyobunsha. Dr. Taniguchi was to meet with an unknown, unnamed young foreigner. A second-generation Japanese American, who worked in the office as the English editor, had been appointed to act as interpreter. However, on the same day, he had rung in to say that he had gone down with a high fever and could not come in. There was a frantic search for his replacement, as a result of which J., who as a youth member regularly had dealings with the editing office, was appointed. J. had been two years ahead of me at university and was proficient in English as he had also studied at an American university as a Fulbright scholar.

I heard from J. later that there had been a slight problem with the actual interpreting. There had been no time for a briefing before the meeting between Dr. Taniguchi and the stranger, so he turned up for the encounter unprepared. Knowing that Dr. Taniguchi had excellent English reading and writing skills, J. assumed that he also had a sound understanding of the spoken word. As a result, halfway through the meeting, J. became so absorbed in what the foreigner — it was Husein Rofe — had to say, that he failed to translate much of it and left out large chunks! (This might possibly explain why Dr. Taniguchi never fully understood Subud.)

This was all speculation in hindsight and the meeting itself proceeded without incident. The following morning, the head of Kyobunsha's editing dept., who had also attended the meeting, told us that Dr. Taniguchi had thought Husein a well-intentioned, upright young man. It was because of this that, at J's suggestion, the young workers in the editing department discussed inviting him to meet with them. A meeting with mainly these young members was then set up and I too took part.

The first time I met him did nothing to arouse in me any interest in the man himself or in what he had to say. He had, so he said, come to Japan to introduce a new kind of spiritual training called the latihan of Subud. He had not given many details, and since the editors had come to meet him based on Dr. Taniguchi's good impressions, the talk centered on more trivial topics such as stories of his travels. I completely forgot all about him the day after the meeting.

However, several days later, J. phoned me out of the blue. He said he was going to see Rofe that evening and invited me to join him. That was surprising, as it was the first time I had ever received a phone call from J. but I was intrigued by his strong interest in him. The way he spoke over the phone made this very clear, and I wondered how he could be so attracted to a foreigner in whom I had had no passing interest whatsoever. But J. was a very talented person who was my senior and whom I respected and that was enough - though it was still with some hesitation that I agreed to go.

When we arrived, I discovered something unexpected. Immediately after the meeting with Dr. Taniguchi, J. had contacted Husein and had actually begun the training (known as the latihan) in this new movement called Subud. So I had been skilfully baited. Aware of my cautious nature, J. had worked out how to get around this. (However, I was later to hear that it was Husein who had picked me out from the group of young editors at the first meeting. He had then asked J. to invite me).

I then learned what had transpired at the meeting with Dr. Taniguchi. Husein had recommended that he try the latihan but Dr. Taniguchi had refused, saying it would be like putting God on trial. I had only come along as J's companion, assuming that I would just listen to what Husein had to say, but instead I now found myself directly in the firing line.

Husein's face wore a more intense expression than at the meeting with the young editors. He explained that the latihan of Subud was a completely new way that made it possible to come into direct contact with the power of God. The words, "direct contact with the power of God," attracted my attention even as I was wondering how best to make my escape. Contact with the power of God was the very thing I had been looking for since the original experience that I had had.

Husein went on to explain: "contact with the power of God, the Supreme Being is possible when the thoughts and emotions are stilled and the mind has become empty. The latihan of Subud makes this possible."

He went on, "when you come into contact with this Power, the soul that lies asleep inside your deepest being is woken up."

Those words seemed to dovetail neatly with the reality I had been searching for all my life.

"Once it has awoken, your soul will become your teacher, your master, and your guide. Because you are in direct contact with God's Power, there are no leaders or teachers in Subud who mediate between you and your Creator – there is no need for them."

This was the bit that particularly interested me. If what he said was right and it was possible to contact the power of the Supreme Being, then of course that is how it should be, I thought.

Once he had finished, Husein suddenly asked if I thought I wanted to experience the latihan. If I did, he wanted me to keep coming back for at least three months. I was very confused by this unexpected turn of events. It was clear that he was asking me if I wanted to start doing the Subud latihan there and then.

"If I empty my mind, isn't there a danger of becoming possessed by spirits?" I asked.

He said "No!" firmly. He added that the human soul was stronger than any evil spirit.

My brain went into overdrive as I looked at Husein's face, which a friend was later to describe as eagle-like. His explanations and answers were all clear to me. But was it right for me to casually put my trust in this foreigner whom I had only met a few days ago? Come to think of it, the only thing I knew about him was his name. I knew nothing about where he was born or what his history was. But then, it was a bit late to be asking, and even if he did tell me, there was no way of checking out the story.

I asked him how many members there were in Subud and he replied, "two hundred or so." I was dumbfounded. Only 200 members in Indonesia, the country of the Founder! With only those numbers, this organization would not be missed were it to vanish tomorrow. Even though small in comparison with sects like the Buddhist Souka Gakai, Seicho-no-Ie had about 200,000 members. If Subud was so wonderful, how come its members were so few?

I was also a little concerned about the Indonesian aspect. Now, if it had been India from where so many spiritual leaders had come in the past, that would have been acceptable; but Indonesia? While circumstances have changed now, for the Japanese Indonesia then was still considered a backward country in the tropics that until recently had been under the control of the Dutch. Most people, me included, knew nothing of Indonesia's superb cultural traditions and arts.

I was too desperate to postpone my answer. What I wanted to say was, 'I'll think about it carefully and get back to you.' But something stopped me. Somewhere deep inside, I felt that if I were to go back home then, I would never have the opportunity to visit Husein again. It was also evidence of how attracted I was to the idea of contact with the Supreme Being.

I decided to try and convince myself with a weak argument. 'If he is adamant there is no danger, I'll take his word for it. And if there is no danger but I also don't get anything out of it, I can just look on the encounter with this gentleman as an exercise in English conversation.' And so it was that in his room I was opened (experiencing one's first latihan is when one is first opened to a Contact with God, the Supreme Being). As I stood, eyes closed, in a relaxed posture, I could hear Husein moving around singing something. J. was also moving about. But I myself felt nothing.

However, I had made a commitment to continue for three months so I visited Husein's place twice a week. On the second, third, and even on the fourth visit, I still felt nothing and stood like a ramrod for thirty minutes, with my eyes closed. Husein must have thought I didn't experience anything because I could not rid myself of tension, so he told me to lie on the floor to receive the latihan.

It is not unusual for people to feel nothing for a while at the beginning. There are many reasons depending on the person, and one of these is when the body is too tense and stiff.

The second time I lay on the floor for the latihan, I felt something like a mild electrical current that ran once, and then again, through my lower back. And then the next time, as soon as I felt the stimulus had grown stronger, an enormous wave of emotion rose up from deep inside me, and before I knew it, I had got to my feet and was swaying and singing at the top of my voice. It was an exhilarating feeling, as though part of myself that had been shut away in a dark place underground had been released and through broken walls had now stepped into a wide, new world.

On the next occasion, I was expecting the same sense of relief. However, while my body moved and sang, I was not able to recapture the feeling of exhilaration. No matter. I had confirmed it in that first latihan. I had finally been able to encounter the very thing for which I had been searching.

The Latihan of Subud

Before I go any further, I should mention a little about the origin of Subud, which will form a backdrop to the experiences that follow. However, I want to make clear that any statements about Subud are my own personal interpretations, and descriptions that I consider may help to throw light on my experiences and develop the story. They are not intended as official explanations about Subud. For those who wish to know more about Subud itself, they may contact the World Subud Association (http://www.subud.org/).

In June 1901, a boy was born on the island of Java, Indonesia. He was first given the name Sukarno. However, soon after his birth he fell gravely ill. An unknown old man who appeared at the doorway advised a name change to Subuh (dawn) after which the boy recovered from his illness and grew up healthy. His full name is Muhammad Subuh Sumohadiwidjojo but he is generally known as 'Bapak' or 'Pak Subuh.' In this book, I'll refer to him as 'Bapak.' 'Bapak' means 'father' and it is used in Indonesia not just to address one's own father but to address any elderly man or one's superior.

Many episodes from Bapak's childhood are already in circulation so I won't repeat them here. What is important to explain now, is that Subud itself began as a result of an experience Bapak had when he was 24. It was inexplicable, but – as Bapak was able to confirm later – it was totally real. This is what happened: one night, as he was taking a walk, his surroundings suddenly brightened as though it were daylight. Startled, he looked upwards, and there, hovering above him was a sphere of light that shone even more brightly than the sun. This light came towards him and entered his body through the top of his head, causing his whole being to shake. Fearing he was having a heart attack, Bapak rushed home and lay down, but now he saw that the light came from inside himself and his entire body was transparent.

Resigned to dying, Bapak prepared to give himself up to the Almighty. But as he did so he found his body moving of its own accord, and rising from his bed, to his surprise his feet took him into the next room where he performed the Islamic prayers twice. His feet then returned him to his bedroom where he fell asleep.

The following night and for a period of 1000 days, he was visited in the same way every night. He had many spiritual experiences during that time and was unable to sleep for most of it. Strangely though, he was able to continue his work during the day just as normal. Later he was made to understand that what he had received could be passed on to others, and that they in turn could also pass it on.

During that period, Bapak was told that in the future, the world would suffer a major war; that this would allow Indonesia to free itself from Dutch control and gain independence; and after that, he Bapak - would travel around the world. This would be heralded by a visit from a foreigner who spoke many languages.

When Bapak was 32, he was to have another life-changing experience. It was something that both Jesus Christ and Mohammed are also said to have gone through — heavenly ascension. Bapak's soul left the earth, transcended the solar system, and traveled through seven layers of worlds that spread far beyond space as we know it. Bapak spoke of how the stars sparkled like diamonds below him as he was distanced from the universe to which he belonged. He then traveled on until he came into direct contact with a Supreme Power which revealed to him the origins of our universe and the secrets of life. He was told that his mission was to tell others who searched sincerely for spiritual contact with a higher Power that this was a new dispensation to the human race. Bapak then found that he was able to pass on to others, the spiritual contact that he had received -

from close neighbours to all who sought it, even though any noticeable spiritual activity was impossible under Dutch rule.

The prediction Bapak had been told about was realized 20 years later. In 1947, after World War II had ended and Indonesia became independent, Bapak officially founded the spiritual association known as Subud. Three years later in 1950, the prediction that a foreigner who spoke many languages would visit Bapak was also realized. That person was Husein Rofe. Until that time, Bapak had not initiated any actions himself but had waited patiently for this to occur.

Rofe was a multilingual prodigy who could speak 25 languages. He had traveled to many countries from a young age, earning his living by teaching languages. The purpose of his search had been to find a leader with true spiritual knowledge. He arrived in Indonesia from Africa, via India. While staying in East Java, one of his language pupils had casually told him of Bapak's existence. He visited Bapak as soon as he could and asked many questions. All of Bapak's replies satisfied his heart and mind and he immediately asked if he could be given the Subud contact. He started doing latihan as the first foreigner to become a member.

Husein stayed in Bapak's house for a year. Feeling it was his mission to inform the world of the existence of such an unusual spiritual training, he sought a way back to Europe by publishing articles in European and Middle Eastern magazines and newspapers.

When he came to Japan, Husein had not yet found a way back to Europe and, because of one of his articles, he had been invited to attend a conference on world religions in Shimizu City, under the auspices of one of the new religions there called Ananai-kyo.

But at the conference on religions, no-one listened to his speech with any interest. It was apparent that the real purpose of the conference was just to propagate Ananai-kyo. Despairing, he returned to Tokyo half way through and sought for religious leaders who might have some instinctive understanding of the latihan and Subud. Hearing about Dr. Taniguchi from Seicho-no-Ie, he had requested an interview.

When Husein was told that Dr. Taniguchi had once experienced frequent spiritual revelations but that these had recently become less and less, he thought Dr. Taniguchi might be interested in hearing about the latihan as a new way to reconnect with one's Creator. And so he met with Dr. Taniguchi and recommended the latihan to him. However, Dr. Taniguchi was not interested. Instead, by coincidence, his lack of interest turned out to be how I met Husein.

Misunderstanding and Confusion

It was through Husein that I came to know about Subud, and while still slightly sceptical, I began to practice the latihan by myself. I soon realized that contrary to what I had expected, indeed there did exist in this world a way to come into direct contact with the Almighty, in the form of a spiritual training. The more I practiced the latihan, the more I was drawn to it. What attracted me most was its unparalleled simplicity and purity.

The latihan needs no preparation. To receive it, there is no need for prayer, ceremony, mental concentration, singing, or music. If you are relaxed, try to feel your inner, and surrender yourself to the Supreme Being, the latihan will start immediately. And as soon as you wish it to stop, it will stop. So it is surprisingly simple; the latihan can occur anywhere, at any time, without the need for any accessories.

Eckhart said that God was the extreme Simplicity – the One. He also said that in the spiritual order of things, the higher you go, the simpler things become, whereas the lower you descend, the more complicated things become. I felt that this could be applied to the latihan as well. For example, when God said, *Let there be light!* there was light. But humans, who are of an infinitely lower order than their Creator, require tools, and machinery, and predetermined processes when they want to create something. But when I wanted to do latihan, it instantly manifested itself inside my being and it was this amazing simplicity that convinced me that it was not something devised by humans but proof of the transcendent workings of the power of a Supreme Being.

Furthermore, the latihan does not arise when the will, passions, and thoughts are active, but will instantly appear once those human elements are put aside. This does not mean that these elements have to disappear; it simply means that they are temporarily placed at the edge of consciousness where they do not become active of their own accord. In this way, the will, the thoughts and the passions are restricted and the latihan continues in a state whereby only the consciousness and the inner senses are fully awake. Of course, it would be ideal if thoughts and feelings could be completely put aside, but in reality this is not so easy. However, the power that works in the latihan will automatically calm one's thoughts and feelings enough for the latihan to be received. This is a state that cannot be forced by one's own willpower, but that can be attained without any human effort whatsoever – and that is one of the major characteristics of the latihan.

This is also what protects the purity of the latihan, because it is human volition, desires, feelings and thoughts that bring impurities into our inner selves. (Just think how pure and innocent are the feelings of a baby whose thoughts and emotions have not yet developed!). The latihan can only arise in a state that is free from the workings of these elements. Because the Supreme Being is the source of all that is pure, this characteristic appeared to me to be evidence that it was indeed truly from this higher Source and that the life force at work in the latihan was from this Power.

It seemed to me that the fact that the latihan can exist in this world is itself a miracle. I was simply overwhelmed at having been given the opportunity to experience it as the result of such a remarkable chance encounter, and was completely oblivious to the future trials and tribulations that were in store for me.

I had had a slight hint of things to come around one month after I started doing the latihan.

The trials begin

One morning, I found a memo on my desk when I arrived at work. It was from Dr. Taniguchi, and it read, 'I want a report on how the latihan works'. I had not told a soul at my workplace that I had started doing the latihan, so for Dr. Taniguchi to have discovered this at such an early stage was surprising, to say the least. I already knew that at his meeting with Husein, Dr. Taniguchi had refused Husein's recommendation to try the latihan for himself. This made a response to Dr. Taniguchi's note extremely problematic for me. Even though I had belief in the latihan of Subud, it had barely been a month since I had started and there was no way I could find the right words to persuade anyone else as to what Subud was about or why I had belief in it. Even now, after I have been doing latihan for many, many years, it is still difficult to explain Subud in words.

I thought long and hard but could still find no answer. I concluded the only way was to try and write in as neutral a way as possible, the procedures of the Subud initiation, or opening as it was called, including what happened to me at the time and how I felt about it.

A response came back from Dr. Taniguchi, almost immediately on the following day.

'The latihan of Subud is identical to the spiritual practice that I experienced in the Omoto Shinto sect. There is a danger here of calling up discarnate entities. You need to stop this immediately'.

In the light of the relationship I had with Dr. Taniguchi, this was equivalent to a direct order. From a management point of view, he was the highest authority over me in the workplace, higher even than the president of Kyobunsha; in religious terms he was the teacher and I, the disciple. From all angles, I was therefore in a position where it was my duty to obey him. However, I had no intention of stopping the latihan. I already believed in it and from my point of view, Dr. Taniguchi's judgment was based on misunderstanding. I was aware of what he meant by the dangers of possession by spirits, as I had read about this in his autobiography. That is why I had pressed the point with Husein when I first started. But I lacked the knowledge and the skills to dissuade Dr. Taniguchi from his misunderstanding. So after much hesitation, I finally resolved not to answer him but instead, to ignore his memo.

I was anxious as to how Dr. Taniguchi would take this and what he might say to me, but fortunately several days passed with no communication from him. But this was not the end of relations between him and me. A year and a half later, they were to resurface in connection with an illness I was to suffer.

The small latihan group that had started around Husein began to grow; mainly centering on J's family and their friends and acquaintances. Gradually, friends of mine also joined until the group was more than ten members. Husein had originally said that if we were to compare the latihan of Subud to a school, it was more of university level than of elementary, secondary, or higher school. He had the feeling that people who could really appreciate the value of the latihan would be most readily found among spiritual leaders who were aware of their own human limitations and realized they had gone as far as they could through will and effort. Husein hoped to find such people to help spread Subud to the world. That is why, losing hope at the International Religious Conference he had originally been invited to, Husein had tried to persuade Dr. Taniguchi. Failing to do so, he concluded that he would not be able to spread Subud around the world from Japan, so he decided to return to Indonesia before winter.

In September, six months after he had arrived in Japan, Husein left in the same manner as he had come; by boat. He had intended to obtain a re-entry visa for Indonesia in Hong Kong, but for some reason was not able to and ended up staying there for two years. In the end, we had spent barely four months in his company.

After we had lost Husein, J. became the group chair and I the assistant to consolidate the group. Everyone supported each other in the latihan. In the previous year, I had married a colleague and she also began doing the latihan. She, along with J's wife, his mother and his sister-in-law, started the women's group. And so it was, that the first Subud group in the world, outside the founding country Indonesia, was established in Japan and appeared to be up and running and on its way.

However, the members at the time, myself included, had many misunderstandings about Subud. While we knew that the latihan was an entirely new method for coming into contact with God's power, we didn't understand the characteristics and process by which the latihan gives rise to purification nor the right attitude to and conditions for the latihan. We simply thought that doing the latihan would advance us spiritually more rapidly than other methods and that we would become spiritually superior to other people. In other words, our understanding of the latihan was firmly within the framework of our knowledge about normal disciplines or meditation.

The group was severely shaken up about ten months after Husein had left. J., the Chair, and the mainstay of the group, suddenly sent everyone a message saying he had decided to dissolve the Japanese Subud group and intended to hold a meeting to that effect on a certain date. This came as a bolt from the blue to me and I hurried to J's house to find out what was going on.

Unbeknownst to me, J. had gone looking for spiritual leaders and gurus to check how far he had been able to advance spiritually by the latihan. He did not understand that to compare himself to others was the very reverse of basic Subud thinking. Astonishingly, he had become involved with the kind of conflicting supernatural powers that were favoured by the wandering ascetics and priests of long ago. He had come across a female guru and, overwhelmed by her spiritual prowess, started to believe quite unquestioningly, every word she uttered. She said that God had told her that since Husein had left, the Subud group had become a focus for evil spirits and needed to be disbanded immediately. Believing her words, J. was now trying to dissolve the group. J. recounted to me the kind of mysterious experiences he had had through her, and as he spoke it became clear that his mind was becoming unhinged. The only thing I could do was try to make him understand that though he was the group chair, he did not have the authority to disband the group of his own accord.

Fortunately, the group general meeting was able to take place in a calm atmosphere, and after the formalities, it was decided that everyone should declare whether they wished to continue doing the latihan or not. While it was pretty clear to everyone that J. was not in his right mind, most of the members did lose faith in the latihan as a result of his attitude and his words. Many of those had joined through J., and when he resigned from the group, there were in the end only four members left, including myself, who declared they would continue doing the latihan. (After J. had left the group, he did actually become temporarily unbalanced and his family had him forcibly hospitalized.)

After that, our reduced four-member group continued quietly with the latihan, but four months later, we were to receive another blow. I had become central to the group but suddenly I collapsed with tuberculosis, and could no longer take part in the gatherings. When it became clear that my recovery could not be predicted, the group was not strong enough to continue and was forced to close down.

Trials and Rescue

My getting tuberculosis came as a shock to me as well as to the other members of the group. At that time we had many misconceptions about Subud and one of those was in relation to illness. We believed that if you practised the latihan, your illnesses would be cured and you would never become gravely ill. Husein had said so himself. But this was definitely a misconception. (Husein had a greater understanding of Subud and had been able to absorb a lot about it while he had stayed in Bapak's house. This gave him a deep insight despite the fact that he had only been in Subud for three years or so, but there were still some areas in which he lacked experience and knowledge.)

It's true that generally, when you practice the latihan, your health improves and the latihan also has a beneficial effect on illness. But the purpose of the latihan is not to cure illness; it is to purify our whole selves so that our souls can develop and fully permeate our minds and bodies. Sometimes, a side-effect is that an illness is cured, but at other times, part of the purification process is that a latent illness is brought to the surface, or as you undergo change, the body can sometimes present symptoms similar to an illness. There are many causes of disease. The question of whether a specific illness is cured by doing the latihan depends on the causes of that illness, the relevance of that illness to the person's process of purification, and what is God's will for that person. It is therefore inappropriate to practice the latihan for the purpose of curing an illness. To cure an illness, one should see a doctor. In those days, however, we held the misconceived notion that as long as we practiced the latihan, we wouldn't get sick.

When my tuberculosis became apparent, accompanied by a high fever, and when I found that the illness would not be cured rapidly, I was at a loss to understand why I had got it. Looking for answers, I wrote to Husein in Hong Kong but he simply replied that he had never experienced such a thing and thought it quite odd.

I was already confused but something else was to happen that was to try me even further psychologically. When he heard about my illness, Dr. Taniguchi announced the following in the Seicho-no-Ie Journal that I had the job of editing:

'Two promising young members of our group were involved with Subud as a result of which, one went mad and the other contracted tuberculosis.'

Although Dr. Taniguchi did not give any names, it was clear he was talking about J. and me. I did not think my illness was caused by Subud, but I had no evidence to prove otherwise, nor did I have any idea as to what had caused it. My mind was plagued with unanswered questions.

I was concerned that Dr. Taniguchi's words would affect my status as a member of Kyobunsha, but more to the point that it would have a subtle effect on my mother's status as both a member and teacher of Seicho-no-Ie. In fact, my mother had been opened in Subud just before J. had left and the group had fallen into disarray, and she had experienced the latihan twice. She then had the dilemma of having to choose between a judgment based on her own experience and the one expressed by Dr. Taniguchi, founder of Seicho-no-Ie. Fortunately she never uttered a word of criticism about me or about Subud.

There was also a financial aspect that worried me. I had zero savings and while Kyobunsha, according to company regulations, had to pay me six months' temporary leave, if my illness were not cured after six months, my entitlement would cease, leaving me with no income. My wife was looking after our first child, and so was unable to work even if she had wanted to. So I found myself in dire straits in both my inner and outer life.

However, it was then that the Almighty reached out to rescue me. Just around that time, a foreign member of Subud had come to work in Japan. By a strange coincidence, my tuberculosis became apparent the evening that I went to meet him. His name was Michael Rogge and he was Dutch. He was working for the Commercial Bank of Holland and had been transferred from the Hong Kong branch to act as deputy manager of the Kobe branch. He had been opened by Husein in Hong Kong one month before and, prior to coming to Kobe, had met with Bapak in Indonesia. He was to spend his first two months in Japan living in Tokyo. It was during that period that he had written to me.

And so on that evening in December, I went to visit him along with another member from the Subud group. Thinking we would have dinner before we met with Michael, we entered a noodle bar close to where he was staying but suddenly, my body felt very hot and I realized that I had an escalating fever. I thought I must have caught the flu. Afterwards, I realized that this was the high fever that one experiences at the onset of TB, when the disease starts to spread rapidly through the lungs. However, I somehow managed to meet with Michael and then went home. The following day, I was unable to rise from my bed.

Michael's visit to Japan was a great solace to me, as I had to undergo a lengthy period of recuperation. All the other Subud members had lost faith in the latihan and left the group and even though he lived in Kobe and I in Tokyo, he was the only person in Japan doing the latihan besides me. I corresponded with him in my imperfect English. During my two years of recuperation, he also supported me financially. Even though I never once asked him for money, he sent funds every month, without fail, as I still had no income. That money was essential for me, my wife, and my daughter – who was born during my illness, to survive. So, whilst I had lost all my friends through illness, I had instead been given a foreigner who was also a Subud member, as a precious friend.

Michael had also written a letter for me to Bapak about my illness. At that time, Bapak would only correspond in Indonesian or in Dutch, and so I could not write to him directly. So Michael received a reply from Bapak in Dutch and sent me an English translation. This is how Bapak had replied to his question.

> *"As regards the question of Mr. Tatebe; whether he may do his latihan at home, Bapak replies that it is permitted if he can stop his latihan without assistance. As to your second question; if he thinks it himself necessary to go to the doctor for further treatment, Bapak thinks so too. In reply to your third question; this illness is not caused by the latihan, but just the opposite. Before he started following the latihan, he had already several illnesses, which were not thought of as a sickness because no pains were felt, whilst in reality the diseases did exist. As a result of the latihan, the illness is really felt as a pain."*

SUBUD – A SPIRITUAL JOURNEY

As advice, Bapak said the following:

"God knows the capacity of each person's individual soul and knows how much each of them is able to receive of God's gift. The advice of Bapak to those who follow the latihan is to leave everything to the Greatness and Power of God. The same applies to Mr. Tatebe. He may leave everything to the Almighty so that God may cure him of his illness and make him healthier than ever before."

I was surprised that Bapak had realised that I had had several illnesses of which lung disease was one, but his explanation allayed my fears. I could understand his statement that my TB had been latent in me before I began doing the latihan. Both my father and my elder brother had suffered from TB and symptoms, such as the colour of my phlegm, had caused me to wonder if I did have TB several years earlier.

However, I took Bapak's advice to leave everything to God somewhat lightly, and did not read much into it. Many religions talk about surrender to God and I was already very familiar with this vocabulary. But I had not recognized the difference between understanding the words in my mind and putting them into practice, nor my lack of complete trust in this Almighty Power. Surrendering to it is both the starting point and the end-goal of Subud, and though I trusted in Subud and practiced the latihan diligently, I could still only understand surrender as a mental concept.

As a result, instead of following Bapak's advice and entrusting the unfolding of events entirely to God, I reasoned that if the latihan had had the effect of bringing my latent disease to the surface, then surely the latihan would cure it. And so I actually became more assiduous in practicing my latihan. I still labored under the illusion that this was what would cure my disease. I wanted to show to Dr. Taniguchi that he was mistaken when he said that my disease was a result of doing the latihan and I intended to re-establish the group as soon as possible. At least if I were miraculously cured by doing the latihan, that in itself would rebut his argument and serve to dispel any doubts. Otherwise Subud would have lost and Dr. Taniguchi would have won. That was my reasoning. Looking back on it now, I can see how very foolish this reasoning was, but at the time, I was oblivious that this was my own self-will and in fact the complete opposite of surrendering to the Almighty.

I refused hospitalisation because I wanted to practice the latihan freely. Instead of sticking to the principle of doing latihan twice or three times a week, I would practice daily, and sometimes even twice a day so that my disease could be cured even sooner. This was a misunderstanding based on the common notion that the harder you work, the more rewards you reap. Progress in latihan however, is determined by God who knows the condition of each individual. It is not something that is controlled by the human will. This is expressed in Bapak's advice; 'God knows the capacity of each person's individual soul and knows how much each of them is able to receive of God's gift.' Instead of leaving this all to God, I misinterpreted this to mean that by doing plenty of latihans, I would be deserving of God's gift sooner.

SUBUD – A SPIRITUAL JOURNEY

To begin with, I applied myself by doing the latihan at home and using the rest of my time to rest and read the Old Testament, the Koran, and other Buddhist texts I had not had the chance to read before. During that period, I had an unexpected experience. It happened on the way back from a nearby clinic where I had gone to receive some medicine.

It was around lunchtime and there was not a soul about. Just as I was slowly making my way down a gentle slope, I was suddenly overcome for no obvious reason, with a feeling of repentance towards God. This was an entirely new emotion, distinct from a sense of regret. I had to apologize and seek forgiveness - not for my past actions but for my present state. I understood that while I was receiving the extraordinary blessing of the latihan of Subud, I could also see how impure was my state and no matter how many times I apologized for this, it would never be enough. It was clear that this was something that had welled up from the depths of my being. On the one hand, I was slightly surprised, and on the other, able to observe myself. At the same time, I wept. I understood then that this was a sincere repentance expressed by my soul.

However, although I had experiences like these, it was clear that my health was not improving after three, four, and even six months had passed. My confusion grew and I began to lose patience. Then, after nine months of daily, intense mental struggle, I finally came to a state of complete exhaustion and gave up. It was then, after much discussion with my mother, that I agreed to enter hospital. With my resources completely depleted and in a state of total exhaustion, I let go of my desire to prove that the allegations of Dr. Taniguchi were wrong. In this state I even relinquished my resolve to re-establish the Subud group – indeed I did not care what happened. I entered a TB hospital in Nakano. What I was to understand later was that this was my first step towards complete surrender to and trust in God. It was not that I had set myself on the path to surrender but that I had been forced there out of necessity. Now I simply didn't give a fig about anything, but I realise now that this was, in fact, my first act of surrender to my destiny and to something greater than myself.

Once I had given up everything and entered the hospital, I relaxed. An examination showed my right lung had two cavities and that the disease had also spread in my left lung, necessitating surgery. At that time, drug treatment for TB had only just started and surgery was the preferred method. Fortunately for me, it was not immediately possible and as my drug treatment progressed, I gradually showed signs of improvement and did not have to undergo surgery.

I spent much of my time reading books that Michael had lent me. These were about theosophy, or by authors who had not yet been introduced to Japan, such as Krishnamurti, Gurdjieff, Ouspensky and so on. I was able to read these books in English because I had so much time on my hands.

I also continued doing latihan at the hospital by choosing places that were not frequented at certain times. Having given up on the idea of re-establishing the group soon, I intended to continue doing the latihan quietly by myself for ten years until I had gained enough experience. I had learned the hard way how difficult it was to try and get others to recognize the value of the latihan.

And then, eight months after I had entered hospital, some unexpected news landed at my bedside. Husein who had been delayed in Hong Kong, had finally arrived back in Britain, and opened John Bennett, who after the death of Gurdjieff and Ouspensky, had taken over the leadership of the Gurdjieff group in England, and Bennett had now invited Bapak to Britain. Things started to develop at astonishing speed and the news came thick and fast. Hundreds of people had been opened in Britain through the Gurdjieff network and the miraculous cure of a famous English filmstar, Eva Bartok, who had received the latihan, was causing a media stir. Bapak had visited Germany and Holland by invitation and had also been invited to the USA and Australia.

For me, these were all unbelievable events. Husein had told me when I was first opened, that Bapak had said he would soon travel the world but I had not believed it for a moment. From an objective viewpoint at the time, no framework existed to allow this to happen and I had dismissed it as impossible. So the simple fact that the impossible was indeed made possible was enough to quicken my heartbeat. The line I had taken, to continue solitary latihans for ten years, looked like it might need some adjustment. But I was still bed-ridden.

In fact, I was not discharged for another seven months. When the time finally arrived and I came home, I thought I had learned patience and was sure that I would be able to handle anything that cropped up in the future. However, little did I know what lay ahead.

Early Spiritual Experiences

The first place I visited after I left hospital was J's house. Even though he had done what he did and left the group, I reasoned that he should have returned to normal and I wanted to check on how he was and what he thought of Subud now.

J. was teaching English at a university. At first, he behaved as though he had completely forgotten everything that had happened in the past but as soon as I told him about Bapak visiting Britain and the spread of Subud to several other European countries, he became very interested. J's father told me that he himself had actually wished to continue doing the latihan, but was forced to withdraw from the group because of his son's deplorable behaviour. J's wife and his sister-in-law were also inclining towards taking part in group latihans, should the group be re-established. And so unexpectedly, I found myself able to re-start the group immediately if I so desired.

However, there was an urgent issue to resolve before I could do that. It was the problem of earning my living. Fortunately,

Kyobunsha had communicated to me through my mother that I was to be permitted to return to work. Not only that, they were happy to tailor my work to my convalescent state for quite some time. I suspected that these were partly Dr. Taniguchi's wishes, and indeed for one so weakened after a lengthy recuperation, it was an unsolicited, extremely generous offer. But I postponed my answer. Eventually, my mother and older brother started to lose patience. Convinced that no one else would employ such a weakling, my brother threw up his hands at what seemed to him like my madness. Objectively, he was right. My mother, who had been living in our apartment since I went into hospital, would start up the debate every day as soon as she returned from work at Seicho-no-Ie.

My reason for hesitating to return to work at Kyobunsha was that if I did so, I would not be able to continue doing the latihan openly and this would also make restarting the group problematic. But my mother simply could not understand why this was so important. She argued that if I wanted to do the latihan, what was wrong with doing it secretly for a while. And then, finally as a compromise, she begged me to go back just for one or two years and then I could find some excuse to leave the company.

Yet still I hesitated. My debates with her just went round in circles.

"If you are so hesitant about going back to work, it must be because you really don't like Seicho-no-Ie."

"That is not true."

"Then why can't you do as your mother asks you?"

"Because I don't want to have to do the latihan secretly."

"If that's what you're saying then it must really be because you're against Seicho-no-Ie."

My mother was now a teacher at the Seicho-no-Ie head office, and Dr. Taniguchi was not only her superior, but the founder of the religion of which she was a disciple, and someone to whom she was indebted for rescuing her from an incurable disease. Until then, my mother must have felt ashamed because of Dr. Taniguchi's pronouncements about my illness. As far as she was concerned, it was obvious that the offer by Kyobunsha was based on Dr. Taniguchi's wishes; for me to refuse would annul his good will and furthermore, could only be viewed as a public revolt against his teaching and authority. If that were to happen, she felt that her only course would be to remove herself from Seicho-no-Ie. I was painfully aware of my mother's position and so, unable to reject the offer outright, could only offer ambiguous answers.

This state of affairs continued for several days until something unexpected occurred. One evening, we had been arguing until two in the morning, and my tired mother had taken herself off to bed while I remained sitting where I was. Exhausted, my head began to feel so hot it was as if molten lead flowed through it, and I could not think or sleep. Half unconscious, I raised my eyes and muttered the name of God.

At that very moment, I felt a gentle vibration and something descended like a transparent wrapping of cloud, enveloping my entire body. My brain felt as if a cool breeze was now flowing through it and in an instant, my head, that had felt so heavy before, became like a blank piece of paper. I felt as though as I was observing my own empty brain. And then, it seemed a voice said, 'Write a letter to Dr. Taniguchi!'

No sooner was that said than word after word started to appear in my brain, as though an electric typewriter were at work. The words arrived at a speed that allowed me to read them, so that as soon as I had finished one word, it disappeared and was replaced by the next. What surprised me was that the words were a letter from me to Dr. Taniguchi. In the letter, I frankly laid out my thoughts on the latihan of Subud. I was saying that it was my intention to continue and to re-establish a Subud group and that I did not feel there was a contradiction between Subud and the ideas of Seicho-no-Ie. Therefore, I had no problem about coming back to work for Kyobunsha, and was grateful for the company's offer. However, it was possible that my intentions could be perceived as problematic to the organization of Seicho-no-Ie or to the harmony of its group. Because of this, I left it up to Dr. Taniguchi's judgment as to whether I should return or not.

It was a fairly lengthy letter. Once I had finished, the transparent wrapping of cloud lifted and I came back to myself.

My mind was filled with a sense of relief. I had no idea of the outcome, but thought things would now improve. I shook my sleeping mother to tell her it was all right, everything was about to get better; but no doubt in her half-asleep state, she had no idea what I was talking about.

The only unfortunate thing was that I put off actually writing the letter until the following day and went straight to sleep. Convinced that the words had been etched into my mind, I was sure I would not forget a single letter. But when at my desk the following morning, even though I remembered the gist of it, my memory of the detail and the exact expressions had faded. As a result, the actual letter I penned was far inferior to the wonderful one I had received.

It was certainly true that Dr. Taniguchi felt something when he read the letter. I finally received his reply: 'You have proved yourself to be honest and I believe you are now being guided by a higher guardian spirit than before. However, since you wish to create a Subud group, I feel it is better that you leave Seicho-no-Ie and carry on with your activities outside.'

Thus, my problem was solved. Nobody in Seicho-no-Ie could complain if I left under the instructions of Dr. Taniguchi in response to my inquiry. My mother's position would also remain intact. I visited Dr. Taniguchi's house along with my mother to make my farewells, and he willingly gave me his blessing.

This solution for me when I had been in such a dilemma was a gift from God. Indeed, you could say that this was my first true spiritual experience since starting the latihan. It was a rare thing to be given every single word of a lengthy letter, from beginning to end, and in fact, I have never received such detailed instructions since. I feel the reason I did get such special help was related to my subsequent re-establishment of the Subud group. The strange experience of having a letter written for me that was both mine and not mine gave me a number of thoughts that served to remove the scales from my eyes on many counts.

First, the idea of writing a letter to Dr. Taniguchi was entirely unexpected and not an option that I had entertained. I had felt that whatever I wrote, to communicate my thoughts in a letter to the Founder would appear as a rebellion against his authority after his pronouncement that Subud was the cause of my illness, and would only worsen the situation. That is why I had not considered it an option. But God's way was different.

Secondly, there was nothing strange in the contents of the letter. While expressing my thoughts about Subud in a frank and sensible way that left no room for misunderstanding, the letter was also imbued with sound reasoning and gratitude. Later, I was to hear Bapak say many times that God is 'normal'.

But what was most surprising to me, was that I had surrendered the decision about my fate to Dr. Taniguchi. To entrust my own destiny to another was not something I had ever thought about. But when I was writing – or rather reading – the letter, I understood that to entrust my fate to Dr. Taniguchi was nothing other than surrendering to God, which was what I had to do under these circumstances.

And that is why Dr. Taniguchi felt something by reading the letter and how the outcome could be satisfying both for me and my mother, and quite likely for Dr. Taniguchi too.

Everything went smoothly after that. Michael invited me to stay in his house in Kobe for a month and we planned to translate into Japanese and then to publish John Bennett's book, *Concerning Subud* that had already been published in Britain. To speed up the publication, we agreed to share the translation task amongst three people, J., his sister-in-law, and I.

When I returned to Tokyo, I discovered that J. had already started preparing to set up the group and was looking for a latihan place. In the meantime, two or three of his acquaintances had joined and a latihan group was established again in June. Since I had not gone back to work at Kyobunsha, there was still the major issue of finding a new job. However, after having undergone all those experiences, I was not too concerned.

Without even having to look for work, an acquaintance I knew only slightly then came to me to say that the patent office where his father worked was recruiting. I was able to start work there from August. The office was an international patent firm of which 90% of the work was making patent and trademark applications from Japan to abroad and vice versa. Thankfully, I had familiarized myself with English at the hospital and after a brief interview with the director, was immediately appointed.

There followed even more unexpected blessings. The patent firm had expanded and was due to move to a new building the following January. Until then, since the office space was so small and there was no place to put a desk for me, I was asked if I could come in only every second day. To me, who had spent such a long time bed-ridden and had still not fully recovered my strength, this was like a wish come true. It was only after I started working that I realized that for a while, I would be so fatigued by even one day's work that I would have to spend most of the following day in bed.

John Bennett's book was translated as *'Subud, A Miracle of the 20th Century'* and published in December. It had been Michael's wish that we invite Bapak to Japan to coincide with the publication. We were still only a tiny group and the prospect of inviting Bapak seemed impossible as we had no funds. However, with Michael's efforts, Bapak's agreement and the support of Subud Britain, we were able to make this a reality.

Bapak arrived in Japan in February of the following year (1959). The book had provoked plenty of reaction from readers and during the five days that Bapak stayed in Tokyo, more than 200 people received the latihan. In this way, Japan's Subud group was miraculously re-established and Bapak appointed helpers and a committee. I should explain that helpers are responsible for opening new members and looking after their latihans, while the job of the committee is to manage the organizational aspect of the group. And so, we started afresh with many new members and I became one of four male helpers appointed.

The Ultimate Inner Experience

For about six months after Bapak had first come to Japan, my days were extremely busy. As a helper I had to support the members' group latihans, provide explanations to applicants, open new members, and assist with setting up groups in different cities. There were not enough helpers but even so it was not meant to be a good idea to appoint people who had virtually no experience of the latihan.

Finally, by summer, the number of helpers had grown and I was able to draw breath. I felt mild fatigue as well as a tranquil satisfaction. It seemed to me that I had fulfilled my responsibility as one of the first people in Japan to discover Subud, and therefore that my role had now ended. Perhaps because I was tired, I felt inside something that was akin to a yearning for death or Paradise. I wanted a rest. However, instead I was to become caught up in a maelstrom of events in the autumn of that year, a maelstrom which lasted over two years and was to become the most significant inner experience of my life.

It began with several mysterious events. They occurred successively and were utterly incomprehensible to me. Looking back, I realized that the story had had its start a year before, when I had finished convalescing and started work in the patent firm. It had begun with the mysterious dreams I had had two nights running; on the night I had visited the patent firm for the interview and on the following night.

In the first dream, I was walking alone down a long, dark tunnel. I could see a faint light ahead and I thought that it might be the exit. When I got closer I saw that the wall on the right was hollowed out to form a small room, where an elderly person with white hair was sitting at a desk facing the pathway. As I passed in front of him, he called out my name. Thinking that he somehow knew me, I stopped, whereupon he gently told me three things.

"Your illness is not your fault. It's because of your blood line." This was his first statement.

"You will become known by twice, even three times more people than those who know you now." This was his second statement.

Then the old man took out two or three sketches and showed them to me. The drawings were that of a young woman and depicted her head and shoulders at different angles.

"It would be better for you to marry this woman," said the old man.

Although the old man seemed to know me, was he not aware that I was already married and had a child? I thought this but did not say so. As he said nothing more, I decided to leave but just as I opened the door, I woke up.

It was a significant dream but I could make neither head nor tail of it. By my illness, he must have meant my TB, but how could that be the fault of my bloodline? As for the old man's second prediction, even if my current small social circle grew three times as much, it still would not be such a big deal as he appeared to make out. But in particular, the final suggestion about marriage: what was that all about? Although he appeared to know about me, he ignored the fact that I already had a wife and told me I had better marry 'this woman'. Why did he come out with such impossible nonsense? No matter how hard I tried, I could not understand it, so I decided to ignore the dream.

However, on the following night I had another meaningful dream. This time, I was in a small, dark room. On a little table there was a lamp, and it threw a faint light on a pile of cards that looked like playing cards, which were laid out on the table. Several people were standing around but it was too dark to see their faces. Other people were trying to get in through the door. The people around the table were stretching out their hands and taking cards. Thinking that I should take a card too before they all ran out, I reached in from behind and took one. I turned it up. On it were written in flame-red letters, the words, 'Enter. Triumph.' The dream ended there.

Here was another dream that looked like it was incomprehensible. However, seeing that the dreams had occurred on the night of my interview and on the following night, I took it to mean that at least the new job was not a bad one. I soon forgot about these two dreams.

Sumiko

A year passed and by the following autumn, Subud was well established, I had gotten used to my job and my mind was returning to normal. It was then that I noticed there was something unusual about one of the women who worked at the patent firm. Her name was Sumiko, and while she was much younger than me, she was my senior at the firm and it was she who trained me.

The unusual thing I noticed about her was that whenever we sat side-by-side to work, I would start to feel unusually calm. But this was no ordinary calm – this was a certain kind of calmness that I had, until then, only experienced in my latihan. I wondered if this young woman possessed some special quality. This happened another two or three times and one evening, after my wife and child had gone to bed, I started doing my latihan, facing the wall of my room. Suddenly, I was made aware that there was someone beside me. I looked around and saw the semi-transparent figure of a woman kneeling with her hands clasped in prayer. It was Sumiko. Of course, it was not her actual body, but rather her astral body that I saw.

While this strange manifestation took me by surprise, it is a basic principle of the latihan not to analyze what one experiences but to simply receive and accept it. I concentrated on my own latihan so that my mind would not be disturbed by this. However, everything was puzzling: how could Sumiko's astral body enter the latihan space when she was not even opened? And how could she appear in a posture of prayer as though she were doing latihan beside me? After a few minutes, the figure of Sumiko started to fade and then disappeared altogether.

The following evening, an even more surprising event occurred. When my wife was asleep, I again started doing latihan in the room next door. After a while, a small sphere of light appeared in front of me. It was probably about the size of a ping-pong ball, but I instinctively knew that it was my soul. I continued my latihan as I gazed on the sphere. Then suddenly, another sphere of light appeared a little distance away. It was slightly smaller than the first sphere and it was Sumiko's soul. The sphere of light hovered for a while and then it slowly approached the first sphere. The edges of both spheres touched and then, like molten metal fusing, they merged into each other to form a pear shape.

At that moment, my mouth moved involuntarily and I found myself declaring, 'Sumiko has now become my wife.' The idea was inconceivable, yet at the same time, expressions of gratitude to the Almighty for this feeling of joy and happiness kept welling up inside me and spilling out. These were like hymns for a marriage.

That was how this experience started. The content of my latihan was utterly transformed. As soon as I was in latihan, whether it was alone or in a group, all that came out of my mouth was songs of joy and celebration for my marriage to Sumiko. There was nothing I could do about it. Sometimes, these songs were in Japanese and, fearful that others in the group would notice, I took care to keep my voice quiet. But my inner self was filled with a latihan of praise for the marriage; whenever I walked the streets and there was no one about, I would just open my mouth and sing.

Then I remembered the strange dreams that I had experienced earlier. In the dream state, I had not paid much attention to the sketches of the young woman's face that the old man had shown me. However, when I looked back, the outline of the face and its features were identical to Sumiko's. The old man had meant Sumiko when he spoke, and his puzzling statement that I had better marry the young woman had now been realized in the form of a spiritual marriage.

In my outer life, a new situation arose in my dealings with Sumiko that corresponded to the events that had occurred in the latihan. The first thing was that I started to feel her emotions. Whenever she felt something – whether it was anger, joy, bewilderment, or the like – I started to feel it inside me as if it were my own. And whenever she directed her feelings towards me, I could feel this instantly, regardless of whether she was in front of me or somewhere else.

What first confused me was that whenever I felt her emotions, I would feel them not as hers' but as my own. It was as if there was no longer a Me/Other factor. When she felt something, that emotion would be accurately reproduced inside me and I would be aware of it - not as specific to her but as my own emotion.

And when I finally stopped doubting that a shared emotional bond had actually come into existence between her and me, all my preconceptions were thrown out the window. The idea that humans led an essentially lonely existence and that the Other is always the Other whose mind can never truly be understood, was completely quashed.

It was only I who was aware of this shared emotional bond as my sensitivities had been made keener by the latihan. Sumiko knew nothing about this but for me it was a startling discovery. When I observed what was happening inside me, I became aware that the emotion I experienced as my own was then directed back at Sumiko who was the originator of it. For example, if it were love that Sumiko felt for me, when that emotion was reproduced inside me, I would feel it as my love towards her. Or indeed, if it were hatred that Sumiko felt for me, then I would experience it as hatred towards her.

This process brought to mind sayings like, 'To be loved by others, you must love others,' or, 'Everything returns to its source.' In religion, there is the idea that the reason human beings can love what they refer to as their God (Buddha) is because they are loved by Him (Buddha). Through my own experience I now understood that this was the truth. As a general spiritual rule or as decreed by the Creator, everything returns to its origin.

But in this situation, how was I to tell if the emotion I was feeling was from me or just a mirror reflection of Sumiko's feeling? After trial and error, I realized I had to remain in a calm, undisturbed state and acknowledge that calm state as my normal one. If a thought or feeling of a different quality were then suddenly to arise for no reason, I could identify it as coming from another person. However, if one's mind is constantly being swayed, and one is seesawing between emotions, it is impossible to make distinctions and all kinds of emotions are unavoidably experienced as one's own.

This shared emotional bond became deeper and deeper as time went on. Sumiko was unaware of what was happening to me. I did not mention Subud or the latihan to her. This was because it was unlikely that anyone could have accepted my experiences – even I myself could not understand them. However, as time passed, Sumiko began to be attracted to me and then came to love me. It became clear that she was feeling something; that there was something special between us.

She told me about unusual experiences that she had had as a child. When she was little, she would often observe strange lights outside the window. And when she was in trouble, she would always be rescued from her predicament by a 'transparent figure.' Once she reached puberty, the experiences ceased, but she told me that recently, she had seen visions in which the transparent figure had returned. The figure was terribly injured, and in the vision she was looking after him with great care. She also said that since her childhood she could not shake off the memory of God telling her to do something before she was born, but that no matter how hard she tried, she could not remember what that something was.

What she spoke about seemed to have some connection with what was happening to me. However, plagued by riddles such as, why there was this soul bond, where it was going to go, or what I should do about it, I felt I could not speak frankly to her. As long as I had no idea what to do, I had to cloak my speech in ambiguities. Since this soul connection had not sprung from my will but from the latihan, all I could do was wait until the latihan gave me the next step.

In the meantime, Sumiko's love for me grew stronger, and I started to experience other strange things. Once, I was surrounded by the scent of heavenly flowers. I had gone to the café in the office building after lunch, to have a coffee. Even though the café was spacious, it was to my surprise filled with the scent of flowers. It smelled like roses and had a heavenly sweetness — as though the café itself had been transported to a flower garden in paradise. I realized that the fragrance was because of Sumiko; for whatever reason, she had become convinced of my love for her and this was the manifestation of her happiness. Though I knew I was the only one who could smell the fragrance, it was so strong and so real, I could not believe that no-one else was aware of it. I was filled with joy, but as soon as I left the café, the fragrance disappeared. In this way, I discovered that emotions also had odours. This was later confirmed by other experiences.

For example, one day, I boarded a very full train to be confronted with a stench like that of rotting fruit. Beside me a young couple were flirting, heedless of the public gaze. The smell was emanating from them. While a faintly sweet scent mingled with the stench, it was so bad I had to hold my breath and I quickly got out at the next station. The stench of rotten fruits appeared to me to indicate the quality of their love for each other.

Another time, as I was passing behind the desk of someone who was absent from work, there was an intense smell of alcohol. The smell was coming from an empty chair. In fact, the person whose chair it was, loved drinking and often reeked of alcohol when he came in. Despite the fact that he was not at the office, the smell of a hangover had sunken into his chair, from where it now emanated. But this was the first time I had smelled it so clearly. I thought that this must be how dogs smell odours of which human beings are not aware. All my senses were heightened around that time, and in particular, my sense of smell. (This was a temporary state and after a while, I returned to normal. Otherwise I think it would be impossible to continue living in this world.)

I also had experiences of a different nature, such as when I heard Sumiko's voice even though she was in another place. I had finished dinner and was sitting with my family when I heard her voice calling my name. The voice was not coming from anywhere around me but was audible inside me. Sumiko called me two or three times. I don't know whether she was actually calling me, or calling me in her mind, but I could hear her voice quite clearly. It is actually a very strange feeling to hear the voice of another person inside your own body. I remembered how when Ouspensky had been receiving spiritual instruction from Gurdjieff, he wrote about being able to hear Gurdjieff's physical voice inside himself. (P.D. Ouspensky: *In Search of the Miraculous – Gurdjieff's Mysterious Cosmology*).

I understood then, that the experience he wrote about was possible in reality.

And then, finally, I had an experience that was to top all the others so far. That day, I had used the director's chauffeur-driven car to go to a foreign embassy to have some papers approved. On my way back, I was sitting in the rear seat relaxing, when suddenly my body felt heavy and I was overcome with a sense of exhaustion. I could no longer even remain sitting, and lay down on the seat. But the feeling intensified, and my body was drained of all its strength so that I could not even lift a finger. It was certainly not a normal state.

Then, my chest started to become bright as though lit up and Sumiko was inside. The feeling I had then was indescribable.

It brought with it a sense of reality that was 10 or even 100 times more intense than the reality one feels towards the things of this world — an utterly heightened sense of existence. Bapak characterizes a true spiritual experience as one where the sense of reality is 100 times stronger than normal. Once one experiences this overwhelming sense of reality, I do not believe there is anyone who would doubt the truth of that experience. This is different from a dream or a vision. In a true spiritual experience, one is directly connected to the spiritual domain — a world that has 100 times more significance than our own.

While the exhaustion had to some extent dissipated, the feeling of Sumiko's presence inside me continued until the car I was in reached the firm. On my return, I realised she would still be at the office. I was curious as to the difference between the Sumiko inside me and the Sumiko at the office. Which one was the real Sumiko? How would I feel when I got back to the office still in this state and talked to her?

When I arrived, she was talking to someone else but she gradually came walking towards me and we exchanged a few simple words. This was actually very strange. The Sumiko that was inside me felt so real, it positively sparkled while the real Sumiko who was standing in front of me had a much fainter, shadowy presence. Yet, even though the real person was faint and shadowy, she could move, walk, and talk like a normal, complete human being. And she was clearly unaware that her real entity had detached itself and was actually inside me.

I suddenly remembered the theory of Maya in India that this world is an illusion, no more than a shadow. Until then, I had had no interest in such a belief, but I began to think that there might be some truth in it.

Sumiko knew nothing of these events, but it is not impossible that they did have an effect on her. The love she had for me became much more intense. From a social point of view, her love was unforgivable. I had a wife and a child, and Sumiko had sensed from the very start that I had no intention to divorce. Despite this, she had decided she would give herself to me and she casually hinted at this.

At that time, we were talking together in a café. Without warning, I was suddenly filled with a burning love for her, and an unexpected thought welled up from my heart; I wouldn't care if I went to Hell as long as I could marry her. I was horror-stricken. Until then, that thought had not crossed my mind. I had always thought that the whole purpose of human life was to remain focused on God and on Heaven, and to never desist from this no matter what happened. Nevertheless, I had had this thought in the core of my body. Because of our shared emotional bond, I knew the source of my emotion came from Sumiko. But as soon as I felt it, I knew it was also my emotion and as such, was shocked at the intensity of it. The words, 'fateful love,' came to me. Certainly, the love between Sumiko and me had been born when our souls were linked through a fate that transcended will. I realized that the kind of fateful love I thought existed only in novels – that feels beyond your power to stop even though you know it leads to your own destruction – truly could exist.

Despite this, I did not make any moves towards Sumiko. To be honest, this was not because I didn't want to marry her. Since our spiritual marriage had occurred, the idea of a marriage in this world was of course, a very attractive one. But in order do that, I would have to either divorce my wife, or elope with Sumiko, or conduct an immoral affair in secret, none of which I was capable of doing.

My wife and I had fallen in love at work. We had gotten married around the time that I discovered the existence of Subud. Dr. Taniguchi had told me to stop Subud as it was dangerous, but I had continued to do the latihan. I finally decided to marry my wife when I thought that even if I took the Subud path against Dr. Taniguchi's wishes, this young woman would still follow me. And indeed, just before we got married, she did start doing the latihan and had continued to stay by my side without complaint, even after I had collapsed with TB, even after I refused to go back to my job at Kyobunsha because I wanted to re-establish the group, and even though we had no idea of how we were going to get by. Like any ordinary couple we had our differences and our quarrels, and sometimes I felt awkwardness between us; but none of these had escalated into a major issue and my wife still trusted me. So I could not betray her, or divorce her. And when I considered the effect such an action would have on the newly established Subud group and my responsibility towards its members, I could not behave in such a way that would draw social censure, no matter what the reason.

I was hoping for guidance from God. As I mentioned before, since I myself did not understand what was going on, I could not give any explanations to Sumiko, and so I took no action. I hoped that the latihan would show me the next stage, and what I should do. Since it was through the latihan that this situation had arisen, I presumed that the latihan would also give me instructions. I waited and waited but my wish was not fulfilled.

I tested. I should explain that testing is a form of latihan. In the latihan one does not ask but surrenders everything to the Almighty. In testing, if a person has a problem that is beyond their means to settle, this can be put to God in the form of a question, after which the person does the latihan. In that latihan, the person should be able to forget their question and their desires and just leave everything in God's hands. (For that reason, only people who have had some experience of doing the latihan can do these tests.) If one can truly enter into a state of latihan after asking the question and surrendering everything to God, it is possible to receive guidance in the form of an answer to that question. What form that guidance, or that answer takes, depends on the person, and how far their latihan has progressed. Sometimes the answer comes in the form of bodily movements – which is the most common – and there are also times when it is received internally or in the understanding.

I calmed my mind and asked sincerely, "why has this happened? How should Sumiko and I be from now on? What is it that I am supposed to do?"

Instantly, the answer came tumbling out of my mouth. That was how I received answers at that time.

"The matter of Sumiko is in God's hands. You cannot know yet what God's will is for you."

This answer was unexpected. While it was somewhat comforting to confirm that God's will was involved, it was basically a denial of the question. Unlike tests I had done until then, I found myself back where I started and in a state of suspense.

After several more months, things took an unpredicted turn. Sumiko started to show signs of change. A conflict between reason and emotion arose within her. Where once she had hinted that she was ready to give herself to me, now she started to revise her thoughts on our relationship; she no longer reacted positively to me and was ambiguous and vague in her attitude. Fundamentally, her feelings for me had been both socially and morally unacceptable. Now, the times are different, but in those days, ethics bound people in a powerful way. I had continually been vague in my response to her and never held out any prospect for the future, and eventually, this internal conflict had arisen within her. Ultimately, reason won, and she made the decision to stop loving me.

She started to avoid me. She decided that she was going to use her will to suppress her love for me and thus, make it disappear. But although she was very strong-willed, to try and suppress the love she felt was a supremely difficult task. That was to be expected. Even if she didn't know it, that love had been born out of the marriage of our souls. And so, this heralded for me a time of suffering. As I shared her emotional life, her internal struggle between will and emotion, now came back tenfold to me.

My emotions began to swing violently. Again, and again, I felt the effects internally. Just as I had started to become accustomed to a tranquil inner life, gained through the latihan, I was exposed to wave after wave of intense emotions which I had no way of avoiding. I suffered bitterly from this. Unable to stifle the love she felt for me, Sumiko then tried even harder to strengthen her will to overcome it, with an even more devastating effect on me.

The will is different from the emotions. In the relationship with Sumiko, I experienced her emotions as my emotions. But when it came to her attempts to use her will to suppress her emotions, I felt it like a physical oppression. The area of my body from my neck to my chest felt like I was being clamped in a vice. Sometimes I could barely breathe, and even while standing on a station platform, was not able to move for several minutes. There was no way for me to escape this state. My suffering was so great, I felt I was in hell.

I wanted to talk to her to explain that the love she felt for me was part of God's Will and therefore not a crime, and that to try and dispel it with her own force was impossible. That way I hoped to escape my suffering. However, believing that to converse with me would cause her love to flare up again, she avoided me assiduously and would not talk to me at all.

Finally, I felt that I could not bear this state anymore. I prayed that my connection with Sumiko's soul be cut off. But my prayers were in vain. I also tried to bring my relationship with her to an end through latihan, but I could not succeed. Even though I had felt as if my connection with her had been weakened at the time, I came back to my former state as soon as the latihan finished. It seemed to me that I was surrounded by an impenetrable barrier, with no way through.

And then, one day, there came a turning point. For some reason, I was sitting in front of a mirror. Suddenly an entirely new thought came to me. If Sumiko's soul and my soul were as one, it did not matter how much I begged God to separate us, it would not happen. And so, there was really only one thing I could do. That was to surrender both my soul, and Sumiko's soul to which it was bound, entirely to the Divine Power of the Almighty. That was a gesture of supreme surrender for me.

I still remember the strange feeling that came over me. Until then, I had been practising the latihan in order to improve my own soul. But now, if I were to give over my soul entirely to God, whatever happened to it would no longer have anything to do with me. Would I then continue to do the latihan? What would I be doing it for? I wondered. The answer, 'to worship God,' was one that I was to discover somewhat later.

However this turned out to be the beginning of the end, for then the situation started to change rapidly; it was as if time had been standing still but had now begun moving, and with incredible speed.

First, my wife, who for the past two years had not been aware of Sumiko's existence, suddenly, for some strange reason, became aware of it and started to question me. I explained what had occurred in my latihan, but needless to say, my wife thought this was crazy and could not believe me. She wanted to run to one of my friends for advice but, to make a long story short, from my point of view, that friend was the worst choice she could have made. I knew that for some time, that friend had had a secret intention to destroy my wife's relationship with me should the opportunity ever arise.

However, I was unable to convey this to my wife. Even if I had succeeded, there was a possibility that she would not have believed me; and besides, I was the root cause of the situation. For some reason, however, my wife, who had gotten ready to go out for just that purpose, suddenly changed her mind.

It is hard to explain what happened over the next few days. Outwardly, nothing happened, but I was enveloped by a strange feeling. It was as if a spiritual drama was unfolding somewhere in the clouds above me and I was the spectator on earth, even though I was unable to see the actual scene. I could feel it but could not influence its process nor be involved in the plot. However, I knew that it had something to do with me and that the outcome would have an effect on the outer world. To exaggerate, it was as if the forces of good and evil angels were fighting it out. Several days passed, with the drama unfolding little by little, every day somewhere in mid-air. Then, one day, when it felt as though this drama was drawing to a close, there was a change in my wife's attitude and she informed me that basically, she would accept what was happening between Sumiko and me.

For three days after that, I was urged from within, to sleep with my wife every night. These times were not the result of desire but were quiet exchanges that occurred in a state of latihan. On the third night, while I was lying with my wife in bed, I found myself in a landscape in a different dimension. The atmosphere was serene, bathed in the pre-dawn light and while the fields in front of my eyes were still dark, I could see mountains stretching far ahead on the distant horizon. A faint blue light from the mountain ridge heralded dawn and everything was filled with a heavenly, majestic calm.

The following morning, when I looked at my wife, I was amazed. Something about her had changed. It was as if light from inside her was now shining in her face. It felt as though she had become a completely different person overnight. While the glow that I could see radiating from her did not last, the feeling that she was now different stayed with me. It was clear that change had occurred within her at a fundamental level. The awkwardness that I had felt between us before had disappeared completely. Our quarrels became infrequent and we started to experience a harmonious relationship as a married couple.

At the same time as my wife changed, I also underwent a transformation. This was in my attitude towards women other than my wife. Before then, whenever I met a beautiful or an attractive woman, I was not able to stop the impulse that I wanted to get her attention or that I wanted to get close to her. Since the general belief is that all men do the same, I thought so too, and never paid particular attention to it. But after my wife's transformation, those thoughts completely disappeared quite naturally. If I saw a beautiful woman, I would think her beautiful but my mind would be moved no further than that. I was amazed, as I had never thought this possible.

Even more surprising, this experience served as a boundary line, after which the shared emotional bond which had been so powerful between Sumiko and me, started to weaken rapidly. Sumiko continued to avoid speaking with me, but the suffering I had felt because of these shared emotions, faded away. The problem had been solved. (Sumiko continued as a single person for some years after that, but eventually got married and was blessed with the birth of a son and a happy life.) But the sensitivity I had experienced towards Sumiko's emotional states remained with me in a weaker form and as something I experience towards everyone.

SUBUD – A SPIRITUAL JOURNEY

This ability, that allows me to feel instantly any strong emotions that are directed at me, has been particularly instrumental in helping me to maintain harmonious relationships with others throughout my life.

Once the problem had been solved, I realized that I would never want to repeat that experience again, regardless of how much happiness was heaped upon me. That is how painful the experience had been. On the other hand, even if I were offered all the happiness in the world, I would not want to go back to where I was before. The gifts I was given through that experience, including my own personal transformation, were too precious for that.

What had happened was both a trial and a blessing. I could not help but consider myself lucky that I had been able to overcome the sense of living on a tightrope for two years, where one false step would send me into the abyss. Nevertheless, I thought that if this experience had been to purify me, and if the latihan could bring such suffering, then how could I go on to recommend Subud to anyone! In fact, I held that thought for several years until I was truly able to realize that God's guidance is in accordance with the condition of each individual and I had no need to be concerned with whatever that person experienced or whatever path they walked.

While my problem had been solved, many puzzles remained unsolved. Why had the souls of Sumiko and me been bound together? Why did I receive that answer to my test? How had it been possible that the bond between us, so unbreakable, was in fact broken and the problem solved? How was it that my wife was transformed overnight? There was plenty I simply did not understand.

The answers to these questions were given to me about two years later, when I first visited Indonesia. At the time, construction was underway for a house for Bapak in the International Subud Centre being established in a suburb of Jakarta called Cilandak. At the request of the international Subud office in the USA, Subud Japan purchased construction materials in Japan and sent these to Indonesia. Together with another member I then went there to see the project, but needless to say, I had another purpose, and that was to visit Bapak. When I arrived, I found that Bapak was living temporarily on the first floor of the guesthouse and we were to stay in the corner room on the ground floor. We had a brief stay of only five days, but were able to enjoy a very fulfilling time; every day we met Bapak and conversed with members of Bapak's secretariat.

On the evening before we were due to return to Japan, we came to say goodbye to Bapak. After some small talk Bapak asked me if I had any questions. While I had not had any particular question in mind at the time, I did not want to waste such a good opportunity, so I asked him three. The final question concerned my recent experience.

I left out the details but the story spanned two years and ended up being fairly lengthy. Bapak's secretary, Usman, translated into Indonesian. Bapak listened quietly and when the story had finished said, "was that young woman a Subud member?" I replied that she was not. Bapak glanced upwards for one or two seconds, and then explained: "in the spiritual domain, that woman was actually your real wife, but in this world, you were already legally married. But because of your patience and your surrender to God, God had mercy on you (and here Bapak crossed his arms one over the other), and exchanged their souls."

With this brief but extraordinary explanation, the events of the past that had been jumbled up inside me instantly fell into place like a jigsaw puzzle forming one complete picture. I understood everything. That was obviously the essence of the matter, and no other explanation was possible. Beside me, Usman murmured, "God makes the impossible, possible."

Bapak said, "you and your wife will have a more harmonious life together in the future." He went on, "there must be a clear distinction made between the spiritual world and this one. You cannot mix what happens in the spiritual world with the things of this world."

This was very precious advice. For various reasons, I was lucky enough to have avoided mixing them. To undergo a spiritual experience and then bring that into worldly affairs as a springboard for action is a dangerously easy trap to fall into for many of those who choose to walk the spiritual path. It often leads to misunderstanding and involves other people in the confusion.

This point, however, does require some further explanation. According to my own experiences, human beings can live whilst straddling the two worlds of the spiritual and the earthly domains; but strictly speaking, this will only apply to those whose souls are already awake.

It appears that people whose souls are asleep lead lives that are restricted to the material world on this earth. This world has its own conditions and laws, and whatever occurs here, including events in the lives of human beings, is controlled and restricted by these conditions. Human beings can use their five senses and the reasoning, imaginative, and logical powers of their brains to study, understand, and use the conditions and laws of this world. Current scientific knowledge is one of the outcomes. However, the spiritual world is governed by completely different conditions, and it is pointless to try and understand it through our five senses and our brains. That is why we cannot know about the after-life.

However, people whose souls have experienced an awakening can indeed have a connection to the spiritual world. While the knowledge one gains through spiritual experience is still limited, people who start living in a way that bridges both the spiritual and the material will be able to discover correlations that exist between these two very different domains.

An important aspect of this, is that not everything in the spiritual world is automatically reflected in a corresponding form in the material world. Therefore, truths or events that belong to the spiritual world can be realized in this world as realities but much later, or even in an entirely different form, or it could be that they are never manifested and have their ending in this world.

For example, while the development of a person's soul can affect that person's life here, this usually manifests as a personality change that is invisible to others. In my case, I had witnessed and experienced my marriage of souls with Sumiko in the latihan, but that was something in the spiritual world. Therefore, the conditions that could allow such a marriage in the material world were missing, and the reality rendered it impossible.

If I had tried to marry Sumiko in this world, to mirror the spiritual union, at the very least I would have ended up hurting myself, hurting my wife and child, and hurting Sumiko. Since I did not do that, God had mercy on me, making the impossible possible in a way that only He can and allowing this world to reflect the spiritual one. Bapak's insight was based on these circumstances.

Once we had finished talking we shook Bapak's hand to say goodbye. And then, as I grasped his hand a sudden vibration passed through me like a shower from above. The vibration was so powerful; I could not even open my eyes during that handshake. But there was a clear distinction between this vibration and the vibration I feel during a latihan. The vibration in latihan is like something neutral and transparent; but the vibration from Bapak that penetrated my being was so filled with a sense of bliss that

I could only think of it as coming straight from Heaven. I feel this was a special blessing that Bapak gave me, in relation to the experience I had told him, as I was never to experience anything like it again.

I had once heard from a Subud member in Indonesia, that separate from the physical Bapak, a spiritual Bapak had a continual existence in some heavenly dimension. Until then, I had not paid this much attention, seeing it as a way of showing respect to Bapak, or maybe just as the member's personal hypothesis. But from that moment, I began to see it as the truth. I have no idea how that could be possible, but the vibration I felt at that time was so filled with sweetness and beauty, that I could think of no other explanation.

Looking back, I can see that this was when I first experienced for myself, something of Bapak's spiritual magnitude. The feeling of exaltation was still with me even as I boarded the airplane. Nor did I feel the least bit fatigued on the long journey home.

Pillar of Light

Following these stormy experiences, I was blessed with tranquil, peaceful days. My attitude to the latihan had changed. Since I had decided to surrender my soul to God, I was no longer doing it out of a desire for my own good. Now, I could practice it with an attitude that was closer to the original purpose of Subud –

to worship God regardless of whether or not this brought one personal benefit.

No doubt, this had been a kind of preparation, and for several years after that I was given many different experiences. The first of these was one that was to clarify for me the essence of the latihan.

It is explained to everyone who joins Subud that the latihan is a direct contact with the Power of God, which will awaken their dormant soul and help it to develop. The word 'Subud' is a contraction of three words: *Susila*, which signifies true human behaviour, *Budhi*, which signifies the divine Power that resides deep in human beings, and *Dharma*, which signifies trust in and surrender to God. It is also explained that the latihan of Subud opens a path for human souls, which is made complete through adopting these three characteristics, so that people can find their way from earth after they die, and return to their real home in the world of true human beings.

People who accept these explanations are 'opened' and become Subud members. But in the early stages, it is not always easy to make the connection between these explanations and one's own experience. At that stage, the explanations people hear are still only abstract concepts, and have not been experienced by the person for him/herself. But later, through what takes place in their own spiritual lives, members gradually understand what the latihan is really about. Members who have been doing latihan for a long time, say that once they had understood what it meant, they could never give up the latihan.

But to get to this state usually takes ten, twelve years or more. Until that point, it is not unusual for people to feel that they cannot make a clear connection between what is a very high goal and the reality of their own latihan. So, a person is truly blessed if they can feel the power of the latihan relatively early on, and experience for themselves the changes that take place within them. In that sense, I could have been called fortunate because I was able to experience my own complete answer to the question, *What is the latihan?*

In those days, the Tokyo Subud Group rented the gymnasium of a boys' high school. It was in a state of major neglect. Several wooden partitions were splintered by students who practiced a martial art and the hinges had come off one of the entrance doors, so that it barely stood upright and the cold winds of winter whistled in through the gaps. We would do latihan in the dim light of one or two electric bulbs, with our overcoats on.

One evening, I had just started doing latihan in this dim light, when I noticed that an enormous white wall had appeared on the far side of the gym. It was about 10 meters wide and after further scrutiny, I saw that it extended right up through the roof of the gym and right down through the floor. There also appeared to be white foam around where it met the floor.

I realized that this was no ordinary wall because it was made of light. But then the thought came that what I was looking at was what I can only describe as the 'foot' of God and I was filled with a sense of reverence. Normally, I would have shrugged off this thought, seeing it as a fantasy or a child's idea of God but, for some reason seeing that enormous wall – or rather pillar – of light in front of my very eyes made me think that this was the mark of God's 'foot', extended right down to earth.

It seemed to me that I was staring at this for a long time. The pillar of light gradually thinned and the far wall of the gym which had been blocked from my view gradually came into sight again. After my latihan ended, the meaning of the experience was not clear to me, but I decided not to try and guess but to wait until the answer came to me naturally.

However, there was a sequel to this. At the next group latihan I felt that I was being surrounded by something. Undeterred, I continued until the feeling became stronger and I then realized that I was inside a kind of cylinder. The cylinder was about 3 or four metres wide – with enough space for me to do my latihan - and it was transparent, so that I could see outside it. The cylinder stretched above my head while also maintaining its width.

I looked up and was amazed to discover that it extended vertically right up above me and way into the distance. In fact it stretched into deep space until what seemed like the end of the universe, and from below, I was looking straight up into what can only be described as an infinite distance. If I concentrated hard enough, I could just make out at the upper end of the cylinder, something hazy that looked like it could be the supreme presence of the Almighty.

This was indeed a strange sight. I was inside a column of light which stretched to infinity above me, yet way in the distance I could make out the very top of it. This would normally be unthinkable. Yet it was pitch black inside. I looked through to see what was outside. Unlike the darkness inside, it seemed to be faintly bright outside. A closer inspection showed that this was due to the light being dispersed by the tiny particles of dust that were floating in the atmosphere. I thought that the darkness inside the column must be due to the intense purity of the strands of light, as there were absolutely no impurities present to reflect the light off. And that was why, I thought, it was possible to see so far into the distance.

The meaning of this column of light then became clearer to me. It was a bridge between humans and the Supreme Being – a pathway through which humans could be at the feet of God and through which He could reach us on this earth. And it represented the true purpose of the latihan.

I continued with my latihan throughout this experience. As I observed this pathway of light I realised that there were absolutely no obstacles in the way; it soared vertically towards the Almighty and I was at the very bottom of it. In other words, I was still only at the starting point of the journey. This was, frankly, a little disappointing, because I had thought that having done the latihan for several years I would at least be several meters along the way by now. But when I looked at the infinite space that extended up above me, that thought instantly disappeared.

The important thing was that I had begun to walk the way that would take me to God. As I gazed on this pathway, I understood that nothing else mattered, and the question of how far I had progressed was so trifling, it was not worthy of concern. No matter how far I walked, He would still be even further away. If that were so, how far I had come was immaterial. What mattered was whether I were walking the path properly and would I continue to stay on the path without wavering. I understood this not as a rationale but as an actual feeling. The truth is, that after that experience I lost all interest in how spiritually advanced I was or was not, which is really, after all, like comparing apples and pears. On a scale of eternity that includes past, present, and future, who can know the real truth?

As I gazed on the column of light, I also became aware that it was absolutely straight and smooth; there were no obstacles in the way. It seemed to me that this showed symbolically that the obstacles our souls meet are not put there intentionally but in fact have their origin in our own selves. The journey to God is purification for our souls. Sometimes in this process, we are visited by trials, like my own experiences had been, so it is not always an easy road. But these difficulties are not inflicted by God. They are impurities that we have accumulated not only from our selves but also from our parents, and even further back, from our ancestors. It seemed to me that the straight column of light was an indication that the pain and suffering we feel is not from God, but is a necessary experience that we have to have in order to remove these impurities.

The pillar gradually faded and my latihan also ended. That was when I first realized that the wall of light I had seen in my previous latihan, and the cylinder of light in this one, were one and the same. I had seen the pillar from the outside the first time and this time I was looking at it from the inside. I reasoned that why on the previous occasion, I had seen this as God's 'foot' was because this was to show me that I was in fact at the very bottom of this pathway to Him.

The experience also proved to me the special nature of the spiritual training that is the latihan - as well as indicating that the ladder from Heaven that is talked about in the Bible and ancient folklore is not just a metaphor or a fantasy but has real existence in a spiritual sense. This is the understanding I took away with me. But of course, this is my personal view; I am not trying to claim that what I say is right or that the latihan of Subud is the only pathway to God. No doubt there are many pathways of light to God in this world that I just do not know about.

A unique characteristic of the latihan that I have not seen elsewhere however, is that this pathway to the Almighty is not just a special reward for human effort and devotion, but is something that is open to everyone who wants it, so long as they have an attitude of total surrender to Him. The fact that this pathway is open does not mean that you get to a prescribed destination in one fell swoop. Just as I saw myself standing at the very bottom of this pathway, the issue is all about being ready for the journey. There is a step-by-step progression that unfolds in front of you as you continue and go through the process. How you accept this and how you judge it is an individual choice and decision.

The Supreme Goal

I am sure that at some stage of their lives, everyone has wondered about the reason for their existence. Why were they born into this world and why do they exist? Many people are aware of the question at puberty. In most cases, the question goes unanswered and the young person launches out into the stormy waters of society, and amidst the business of everyday life forgets all about it. But there are also a small number of people who carry this question somewhere inside them for the rest of their lives.

When I was younger, there was a poet I used to like called Rainer Maria Rilke. One of his poems, the *Duino Elegies* begins with such a question.

Why, if it's possible to spend this span of existence as laurel, a little darker than all other greens, with little waves on every leaf-edge (like the smile of a breeze), why, then, must we be human and, shunning destiny, long for it?.

(The Ninth Elegy)

In fact the *Duino Elegies* were too difficult for me to understand, but for some reason, this single stanza stuck in my memory. This was probably because I was so pessimistic at the time; it seemed to fit the very question I had in my own mind. The experience I have described in the Prologue directly prompted my quest for God, but no doubt there were thoughts like these deep behind it.

In 1963, about one year after experiencing the pillar of light, I had a conclusive experience in relation to this question.

The arrow that pierced my heart

There are events in people's lives that even though rare, can radically transform a person's destiny in an instant. The event I am about to relate to you now was one of those. It was indeed a once-in-a-lifetime experience in that it literally changed my life's direction from that moment on.

That morning was a normal summer's day for me. I had gone to the office as usual and started my work. At ten o'clock, I finished the first lot of work and paused to smoke a cigarette. It was just when I was about to start on my next task that, completely without warning, the right side of my chest was pierced by an arrow from the spiritual world that came straight towards me. It penetrated my heart, exited from the left side of my chest, and then disappeared into empty space. It was over in an instant. I felt a sharp pain in my heart and at the same time, the wound poured not blood, but a liquid that was filled with a sweetness that permeated my entire body. My consciousness was filled with a sudden, instinctive understanding. This too lasted only an instant but in this case it revealed to me the eternal purpose of my soul.

I am not in the habit of keeping a diary. But because the revelation that had filled my consciousness was so unexpected, I wrote it down in English in a memo. (The reason I wrote it in English is because the content seemed so far removed from reality that I did not want anyone who came across it to understand it.) It was in the form of a prose poem that expressed the shock and emotion that I had experienced. It went something like this:

Finally I understand! From the very beginning, my soul has been continually searching for its supreme goal. This supreme goal will remain unchanged whether it is in this world or the next. For as long as God allows my existence to continue, this goal will remain unchanged until the end of time.

Now, it is revealed to me: I am to become the lowly - lowliest - servant of God.

Until then, the thought of aspiring to be God's servant had never entered my head. To my mind, the concept was strongly related to Christianity and the thoughts of a priest or minister — not something that had a connection to me personally. Not only that, but the method of this revelation had been so extraordinary: the thought of an invisible arrow reminded me of the Greek legend of Cupid whose arrows cause their targets to fall in love. That is a legend of course; but I came to realize that there was such a spiritual reality, that it did exist and that it was no mere fancy. It was clear from the pain I had felt in my heart and the liquid sweetness that had filled my body, that this was not a delusion.

Later, I found out that St. Theresa of Avila in the 16th century had described being pierced in the heart by an invisible arrow and of entering a state of ecstasy; but I was not aware of this at that time. It is not my intention to compare my experience with hers' but only to show that such an experience has a reality to it.

I was overwhelmed for a while. But then the pain in my chest began to ease leaving only a feeling of bliss. This lasted all day and on the following morning it still reverberated faintly within me.

The understanding I had been given from this experience had an immeasurable effect on me. I was shown with absolute clarity, the reason for my existence. To become the servant of God had been until then, an unfamiliar concept but now it became the whole purpose of my life. From then on, my chief preoccupation was how I could become God's servant. This was because while I had been shown my soul's purpose, I had not been shown how to go about realising it. All I knew then was that it was no good just calling myself, 'the servant of God'. Also, while it is possible that without being aware of it someone is used by God as an instrument for His purpose, to be a servant of God should be different from such cases. First, God Himself had to acknowledge me as such and then if He did so, I had to be in such a state that I could correctly receive His will and instruction.

Looking back now, I can see that I had absolutely no idea at the time just how nigh impossible a task this was. To become a servant of God is the highest goal a human being can pursue. While of course, I did not think that its achievement was an easy task, I was secretly hoping for the next sign from God. But instead I had to wait a long, long time. Thirty years later, I finally had an experience related to this goal, which I will elaborate on later.

Pertinent to the experience was the fact that the memo I had written had not simply stated that my goal was to become a servant of God, but that I had to become the lowliest servant of God – and this word 'lowly' was repeated in order to stress that to become the lowliest servant of God would be my supreme goal. I understood just how small I was before God and simultaneously, was painfully aware that no matter how much time passed, I would remain this microscopic existence for all eternity.

This was a valuable realisation as it helped me to suppress any arrogance in my life. I also discovered that the feeling of utter humility – as though one is nothing - is always present when one is given a glimpse of God's existence. This feeling is like a litmus test that lets you know if you have actually had an experience of God, or not. If you do not feel that emotion, I think it can be said that you have not had a true experience of Him.

Several months later, I discovered that on the day I had that experience, the 9th July 1963, the second World Congress of Subud had opened in Briarcliff, a suburb of New York. The congress had actually started on the evening of the 8th of July but with the time difference, this worked out as the morning of the 9th, Japan time. I had not been able to attend and so had forgotten all about it. But it was interesting to me that on the evening of the 8th July, Bapak had given his first talk. In it he had apparently said that helpers (in Subud) were Bapak's helpers. Assuming that Bapak had started the talk at the usual time of 8.00 pm., I had received this experience some time in the middle of his talk – despite the fact that he was thousands of miles away. Of course, this could be dismissed as coincidence, but the experience had come to me like a bolt from the blue and the fact that it happened at the same time as the World Congress suggested there was some significance in this. That was the first time I had a strong interest in a World Congress and I was determined to take part in the following one.

Bapak Muhammad Subuh Sumohadiwidjojo, the Founder of Subud

Dr. Taniguchi, founder of the spiritual movement Seicho-no-Ie

Husein Rofe, who first brought Subud to the West

Rozak with his wife Muftiah, and his daughter Halimah

Rozak Tatebe

Section II

Various Experiences

Bapak's Spirituality

What I am about to relate concerns three experiences about Bapak that I was given between 1964 and 1967, ten years after I started doing the latihan. Bapak died in 1987 and soon after, people who had been close to him began to share their personal stories of him. I also had many memories of Bapak and it could probably be said that in some sense, my latihan life had chiefly revolved around him. However, the three experiences I am about to recount do not relate to the physical Bapak who I met while he was amongst us in this world, but rather are to do with the spiritual Bapak – the invisible spiritual entity behind the physical Bapak.

The Inner Bapak

For early Subud members, the question of just who Bapak was, held great fascination and there was speculation that he was a reincarnation of the prophets of the past. Bapak himself consistently maintained that he was simply Bapak – a human being charged with the task of being the first to bring God's gift of the latihan to the human race – and he did nothing to change this position. However, for those early members who were in close contact with him, it was clear that Bapak was no ordinary mortal.

Bapak took this stance because for people to receive and carry out the latihan of Subud, it was not necessary, and indeed better not, to know the answer to this question. I suppose this was because he thought that if it became necessary, or that the time had come for someone to know the answer, he or she would find out for him/herself anyway through his/her own experiences. If Bapak were to start proclaiming who he was, then of course, the question of whether to believe him or not would arise; on the other hand, if someone came to know who Bapak was through his or her own experience, even though this person would believe, there would be no need for others to believe. This would avoid creating a problem which had nothing to do with the latihan itself.

Further to this was the issue of making someone into an idol. In the beginning, Bapak advised people not to place a picture of him in the latihan hall. This was to avoid people turning their attention to him rather than to God. My first experience of the 'spiritual Bapak' was related to these matters.

In fact, I first experienced Bapak's specialness on my initial trip to Indonesia in 1963. In my chapter *The Ultimate Inner Experience*, I wrote that I had asked him three questions but I did not mention something that came up at the time, which was the question of Bapak's photograph. At that time, we did not hang a photograph of Bapak in the latihan hall as he had asked us not to. However, I kept a small picture of him on the wall of my bedroom and I often used that room when I was doing latihan alone.

On one occasion when I had been doing latihan there, I became aware of something odd. Latihan is normally carried out with the eyes closed. The body moves naturally, usually to walk around the room. As long as your body is being moved in a latihan state, it is rare that you will bump into anything. So until your latihan finishes, you have no idea where you will end up or which direction you will be facing. What I thought strange was that whenever I did latihan in that room, at the end of it I would find myself standing directly in front of and facing the picture of Bapak. This happened too often to be coincidental. I would often end with my head lowered and my body bowed and whenever I did so, I would open my eyes and find myself right in front of Bapak's picture as though I were bowing to it.

My first question to Bapak in Indonesia had been, why was this so? To my understanding, while this was indeed a picture of the Bapak whom I respected, it was no more than a picture. Indeed, it was actually just a sheet of paper. Therefore, there should be no connection between it and my latihan. So why, (contrary to my own will) did I often find myself finishing up in front of Bapak's picture? That was my question.

In response, Bapak did not attempt to answer the question directly, but had this to say.

"You will one day, find Bapak inside you. Then, there will be no need for a photograph."

Strictly speaking, Bapak's words did not actually answer the question. This was a niggling issue for me but I had a more important question I wanted to move on to and so I let it go. Looking back on it now, I think that the question can also be viewed in the context of images of worship in Buddhism, and in Christianity.

But I did not think too deeply about it at the time. The only reason I had asked it was because it was the first thing that came to me when Bapak had asked if I had any questions. What I had really wanted to ask about was the third question, about my Ultimate Inner Experience.

I did not pay much attention, therefore, when Bapak told me that one day, I would discover the Bapak inside me. I thought that it meant that in the future, I would have a new experience that would bring me closer to Bapak. I could not imagine exactly what kind of experience that would be, but since it was to be sometime in the future, I thought this might be several years later. So without too much thought, I filed it away, came back to Japan, and half forgot about it. However, it was only a few months after I returned, that Bapak's words were to become a reality.

One evening, I was lying on top of my *futon*, thinking it was soon time to sleep. Suddenly, I felt as though I was illuminated by a bright light shining from inside me. In the next instant, I became aware that Bapak was there, within that dazzling radiance inside my chest. It was entirely unexpected, and I understood then that Bapak had said these words, not as a symbolic thing but as the simple truth.

It was a wonderful and very real experience that left no room for doubt, because I had felt something like it once before: when I discovered Sumiko within me. I wrote earlier, that I had felt at the time that the Sumiko within me was 100 times more real than the one that actually existed in this world; and now again I had exactly the same feeling. The only difference was that this time, my chest was filled with a more dazzling and brilliant light and I felt totally enveloped by it as though I were in some heavenly place.

I was experiencing this blissful state while still alive, it seemed. I was living in both worlds; this one and in that heavenly world, and if that state were to last forever, how amazing it would be. But of course, that was not to happen. After about a minute, the Bapak within enveloped in light began to fade.

The experience had disappeared as quickly as it came – but through it I was given an understanding of a small part of Bapak's spirituality – his inner nature. Presumably unlike the physical Bapak, the spiritual Bapak also existed within me, and could be found within me. And if he existed there, I realized this meant that he existed within others too, as long as they met certain conditions. This was as much as could be inferred from my own experience.

The direct result however, was that I was freed from envy towards those who actually lived near Bapak and were able to be close to him. No matter how far geographically I was separated from him, I knew that I was always connected to the spiritual Bapak through my inner self.

The Outer Bapak

The second experience I was to have in relation to Bapak's spirituality occurred one year later, and was triggered by the actions of one of the members.

In Subud, the role of a helper is to explain about Subud to applicants, to give the Subud contact (known as the 'opening') to new members, and to provide advice and help to these people once they have joined.

Helpers are not teachers, nor are they leaders. One of the roles of a helper is to take responsibility for the latihans at the local group they belong to. As Bapak explained, if you were to compare it to a school, the helpers are not the teachers, but those who help to ensure everything runs smoothly by setting up the desks and other equipment. The teacher is the Almighty, and the lessons that people are given by the power of God are tailored to each individual in accordance with his/her own conditions. A human teacher is not required and indeed, would only serve as an obstacle. If teachers were to interfere with the way in which lessons are given from the power of God, instead of helping, they would only serve to hinder the progress of the students.

An issue about this arose when I was looking after the latihan at a local group. One of the members there began to ignore the principles of Subud, and to act like a teacher towards other members. The problem was complicated by the fact that that member had come back from Indonesia where he had stayed in the Subud International Centre for a long time. I later discovered from Bapak, that in fact, he had been going through a form of crisis. What is meant by 'crisis' here is a state that results when someone desiring to speed up their progress does too many latihans, whereby they are affected by intense purification; this sometimes manifests itself as spiritual experiences and an unbalanced mind.

In reality, a crisis can take many forms. Sometimes, the departure from normal behaviour becomes obvious; sometimes there are no outward signs. After a certain time, that stage finishes and the person returns to their normal state. This is an extremely simplified description. Further elaboration is not central to the theme of this book, so I will just say that while people do have crises, these are extremely uncommon.

While on his visit to Indonesia, the person in question, wanting to progress rapidly, had spent a lot of time in the houses of helpers in Bapak's secretariat and had been doing latihans and testing things that were beyond his capacity. As a result, while his sensitivity and perception were heightened, the power of the latihan that he received exceeded his capacity and the impurities deep within him came too rapidly to the surface, triggering a crisis. This manifested as a confused state in which his perception, desires, and fantasies were all mixed up with a sense of superiority - though he was not aware of it.

He had not yet become a helper but considered himself to have achieved a higher state of spirituality than anyone else, and so he started to criticize while at the same time behaving like a leader. He claimed to be bringing new knowledge straight from Bapak and many members who were still inexperienced were taken in by this.

What was worrying for me was that I was responsible for the group. While he displayed enormous perception when talking to the members, his behaviour was erratic and clearly outside the framework of Subud. He was particularly hostile to me who was looking after the group, and he did whatever he could to block me. Often, when I was about to address the members, I would feel an intense animosity from him and would be unable to speak. But I knew there was nothing I could say while he was in that state. All I could do was make a real effort not to be shaken by or react to the feelings he directed at me. I had heard that the best way to deal with people like him was to remain calm and unruffled. This would help to shorten the length of what he was undergoing, and bring him back to himself.

However, this state continued for two and then three months and even appeared to be worsening. I found it harder and harder to bear the tension and it became painful to attend the latihans of the group he belonged to.

But gradually, the outlet for these feelings altered, and I found myself starting to direct them at Bapak rather than at him. Why had Bapak let him come back to Japan while he was in such a state? A feeling of blame towards Bapak grew in my heart. Bapak would have been well aware of his inner state and of how he would behave when he came back to Japan and also of the consequences. Bapak also would have been able to come up with a way to prevent this, or would have been able to postpone his return until he was back to normal. Instead, Bapak had done nothing but had approved of his return and I had to suffer. So it was that I now found myself blaming Bapak.

One day, when I was waiting for latihan to begin, I felt this member's animosity for the umpteenth time and could stand it no longer. When it was time to stand up, I called to Bapak in my mind without thinking.

Bapak, why did you let him come back to Japan in this state? You must have known how much chaos this would cause but you didn't try to stop it. Why?

Then, I'm not sure how long after latihan had begun, I was suddenly aware that Bapak was standing in front of me. His features were hard to distinguish, but it was definitely him. He stood, motionless, and I continued my latihan in front of him. Then, something odd occurred. Without warning, the area around Bapak and me started to shift, and before I knew it, the world around me began falling rapidly away. Soon, the surroundings were moving with dizzying speed, and it was as though I was watching a video in fast-forward. Immediately, I became aware that rather than the world around me falling away, in reality it was we who were ascending. It was like being in a high-speed glass elevator looking out and instead of the elevator going up, it seemed as if the world was falling away from under it.

This went on for some 20 or 30 seconds and then suddenly the surroundings stopped moving. It seemed I was in another dimension. For some reason, Bapak was nowhere to be seen. Instead, empty space stretched out in all directions. It seemed that the members I was doing latihan with had also disappeared except for one – the troublesome member appeared to be lying alone and asleep at my feet.

This was a world ruled by harmony and unity. In that realm, there was harmony amongst all things and all things were bound by a single connection. It was a world of oneness. I looked at the member lying on the ground. He and I were also bound together, as soul brothers. I looked around and I felt the power coming from Bapak stretching to all corners of that vast universe, and everything there was filled with his power. What I thought and felt as I gazed on this scene was that nothing happened on earth without there being some connection to this spiritual universe, and as long as this spiritual universe was filled with Bapak's power, everything that happened, did so only because Bapak allowed it to do so. This thought went beyond reason. I understood that whatever was allowed to happen did not by necessity have to be good either. Bapak's capacity was to be courageous enough to allow undesirable events to occur, without trying to interfere.

With this thought came the realization that Bapak's behaviour was extremely close to God's behaviour. Despite the fact that the power of God is present in the entire universe, and that God is omnipotent, He allows the most pitiable events to occur on earth, without interfering. Was this not the same as with Bapak?

I felt somewhat confused. Did this not mean that Bapak had the same attributes as God? Since it was beyond my understanding to comprehend Bapak, I decided it was better not to think about this any further. These were my thoughts while I was in that other dimension.

When I returned from that other world, I thought I would come back by the same route and that this would involve seeing the world around me rise up as I descended. In fact, this was not the case. All that happened was that the scenery around me started to blur and I came back into my normal latihan state. Presently, my latihan ended. I opened my eyes and I was standing in the room with the other members.

This experience gave me fresh insight into Bapak and left a deep impression on me. While previously, I had indeed experienced Bapak's greatness, it seemed that he was something even beyond what I had understood. But just as I had felt in that experience, I gave up the idea of thinking about it any further. I realized that this was simply beyond my capabilities.

What this experience also gave me was the understanding that beyond this world, there actually existed a spiritual world that was far superior. While I did not know for sure how to position this spiritual world I had seen, it was certain that it had a harmony and unity to it that was what Heaven must be like for humans. It might be what Bapak had called the world of true human beings. Out of the blue, I had been able to experience its existence through Bapak.

(*Note) This is a major conundrum that has been questioned throughout the centuries. If God exists, why does He allow so much terrible pain and suffering? This problem is deeply related to the issue of the free will that humans have been granted. In one of his talks, Bapak mentioned that free will is God's greatest gift to humans; not even the angels have been given this godly attribute. At the very least, it means that humans are given the authority to act and control their environment like gods, as far as their earthly life is concerned. However, depending on how it is used, free will gives rise to evil as well as good. Because of the privileges that humans enjoy, we have been given the potential to rise even higher than the angels but also to be more cruel than the Devil, plunging ourselves and others into a Hell of suffering. That is the meaning of freedom and the price we have to pay for its misuse. Our Creator cannot be blamed for the wars, poverty, discrimination, and other disasters human beings bring down upon themselves. Humans must take responsibility for what

they themselves have created, and must find their own solutions. As a consequence of abusing free will, life on this earth is filled with dangerous temptations. These can debase some people to a lower than animal existence. Bapak intimated that this potential in humans for greatness as well as the danger of its opposite, are a result of God's fairness to angels and other creatures of creation that, unlike us, have not been given free will.

However, illness, natural disasters and many other forms of suffering not created by man, also exist in this world. A central concept of Buddhism is the idea that this life is one of suffering, whether it is ageing, sickness, death, or life itself, and the quicker one can leave it the better. But one might say - if a Creator does indeed exist, why does He allow such suffering to be visited on mankind? In response to this, Bapak said that this should be accepted as a form of testing for mankind. How humans accept and respond to this suffering is a test and an opportunity given to them to develop their soul.

In the Christian religion, the *Book of Job* from the Old Testament deals with this question, head on. Job was a pious man who had a strong faith but who was visited by all manner of catastrophes. He blamed God and called on Him to answer why he should have to suffer so much when he had done nothing to deserve it. His friends tried to persuade him that he must have done something wrong, but Job claimed that he was in the right. At the end of the *Book of Job*, God responds to Job's 'Why?' question, but not in a very satisfying way. Instead, He lists examples of His greatness and excellence and says all humans can do is to try and second-guess God's will.

However, at the very beginning of the *Book of Job*, there is the story of how God and the Devil made a wager as to the strength of Job's faith. The disasters visited on Job were a form of temptation by the Devil to see if he could wean Job off his faith in God, and were also tests from God to demonstrate how unshakeable Job's faith and belief really were.

Another way of looking at this problem is that the existence of suffering is fundamental to human existence on this planet. The earth we live on is basically, a material world. So for matter (such as minerals, for example), earth is home, a domain where they will exist for always. But in the case of plants and animals, and more importantly, humans, while they have a material form, it can be said that their essence (the life force or the soul within them) does not fundamentally belong to the material world. In other words, from a spiritual point of view, plants, and animals, and humans have their true homes in the spiritual realm which transcends the material world, and life on earth is a temporary one that allows them to experience living in the material world.

Because of this, plants, animals, and humans cannot live forever in this world as material objects do. This leads to the concept that it is the limitations of the body, clothed in flesh so that it can live in this world, that gives rise to suffering because the body can never be fully compatible with the material world. No doubt, suffering is also part of God's plan in that His Divine Providence allows us to end our experiences on earth and return eventually to our true home, and not make the mistake of thinking that the earth is our final resting place.

While I have been describing my understanding of these ideas, the reality is that they are beyond my personal experience, and as such, I am not able to answer this question myself. What I have written is based on Bapak's talks, as well as on the understanding I currently have in my mind, and which is therefore still hypothetical. But I would like to introduce here an article I read about an interview with Mother Theresa that I found deeply moving. In the interview, Mother Theresa had explained in relation to God's existence, that poverty was man-made and not God's responsibility. The female interpreter had then refuted this, saying that the world was filled with suffering. This was Mother Theresa's reply:

"Suffering is not the same as poverty. Suffering is not something that we can understand with our human intelligence. It is an extraordinary arrangement by God and it cannot be explained. But there is one thing that I know. When human beings suffer, God stays with them, like a kindly father."

(Collection of interviews from the Daughters of St. Paul, Encounters with Mother Theresa).

Bapak's Mission

As a result of the experience of other dimensions that I have mentioned, I thought that I knew everything I could know about Bapak. But there was more to come. This happened at the Third Subud World Congress held in Tokyo in 1967.

Subud World Congresses are held once every four years. These days, up to three thousand people attend these Congresses and they come from many countries around the world. The Congress usually lasts for ten days or more, and the pre-congress logistics of finding accommodation and venues are complex and costly. However, in those early years, only a small number of members used to attend and the total number of people who came to the Tokyo Congress was 400, with about 250 of these from overseas. Subud Japan was able to cope with the logistics for this Congress because the scale was still small. It was held in and around the Yomiuri-land Hotel and facilities in the suburb of Tokyo.

It had been decided that the official language was to be English, and the talks that Bapak gave during the Congress were to be translated into English with Japanese translation available only at designated times, to avoid further delays. (Today, simultaneous translation is always available at these Congresses.) My role was to interpret from English to Japanese. This meant that not all of Bapak's talks were translated into Japanese, which was unfortunate for those Japanese members who could not understand English, but fortunate for me, as I found translating Bapak's talks required a great deal of concentration. This was partly due to the difficulty I had in understanding the spoken language as well as the fact that translating Bapak's talks requires more than an ordinary reliance on memory.

When Bapak gave his talks, there was no preparation. He would say whatever it was that he 'received' from God to say at that moment. None of this came from his brain. So whenever I tried to memorise what he was saying, I just could not retain it and my mind would go completely blank. For those who have not experienced it, this may be hard to comprehend, but if in the middle of interpreting something the interpreter starts to use his thinking, no matter how infrequent this thinking may be, what happens at that moment is that the mind loses grasp of what is being said and goes blank, inducing a state of panic.

When Bapak visited Japan on his second trip and I was the only interpreter present, I was warned about this by Usman, who used to accompany Bapak and interpret for him. In fact, he said that on one occasion in Europe, a woman who was a fluent English speaker tried to interpret Bapak's talk, but she could not translate even one word and ended up crying on the stage.

So what was required for the translator on these occasions was not to attempt to memorise the words but instead to relax, as when in latihan, and without using the mind, listen and understand whilst in a state of inward consciousness, and then render that understanding into Japanese, or other languages. While I used to try hard to do just that, things did not always go smoothly. To continually interrupt during the interpreting in order to clarify something, would also hamper the fluidity of the talk. And so it was that despite the fact that I had often translated Bapak's talks, trying to maintain a latihan state while also concentrating hard, was something I found exhausting.

The first time I interpreted for a Bapak talk, I had an experience that remains with me to this day. I had had a latihan beforehand and during that time I had felt a vibration suddenly concentrated on my mouth. This was the first time I had ever felt a vibration concentrated in one single part of my body. Finally, my entire mouth was filled with this vibration. Since this was the only part affected, I later felt that my mouth was undergoing something unusual, so that I could better interpret Bapak's talk. In other words, the interpretation of a Bapak talk was a very special task.

One day during the Congress, a talk by Bapak was scheduled but there had been no instructions for Japanese interpretation. Inside myself, I was relieved. Perhaps it was selfish but it meant that at least that day I could relax and listen just for myself. The thought made me happy. I took a seat close to the back and waited for the talk to begin.

At last, Bapak and Usman appeared on stage. And then, as Bapak began to speak, I felt a strong vibration. The vibration was stronger than I had ever experienced before. This was strange as I was not actually doing latihan, and so I reasoned that the talk must be of special importance and the vibration must have been related to that. However, after a few minutes, Bapak suddenly stopped and said something to Usman. Then Usman stood up, and I heard him calling my name in a loud voice. Bapak had indicated that the talk should also be translated into Japanese. But I did not want to keep interrupting Bapak's talk in front of so many people from so many countries.

I got up and took my time in walking towards the stage, all the while hastily trying to change the joyful feeling that I had formerly had, that I too could take part in the testing. Fortunately, by the time I reached the stage, I was ready to interpret.

I sat down beside Usman and the talk continued. And then I had my own special experience - whilst Bapak was still talking. As I did not understand Indonesian, I had nothing to do while Bapak spoke until the English interpretation began. As I was listening to him, I glanced at his profile. It was at that very moment that I felt I had been hit by lightning. It was as though a sudden flash had pierced the darkness, and lit up Bapak's figure so that everything around him appeared fading into darkness behind him. Even so, this figure was somehow not the ordinary Bapak, but the Bapak sent to Earth by God as the representative of God's Power in this world. This scene faded in an instant, and everything on stage that had been in darkness returned to its normal lighting. Bapak continued to talk as though nothing had happened, and I concentrated on my role as interpreter again.

This experience had a decisive effect on my life. It was one of those split-second moments that have a life-changing impact on one's future. To truly explain why this should be, I need to go back to an experiment I embarked on four years earlier after I had been given an understanding of my soul's supreme goal.

I have already spoken about how I felt it was my life task to discover a way to become God's lowliest servant. So to help me do this, I now decided to start a welfare project. Since the Almighty does not need any help from mankind, there is no service we can do that will help Him directly. But what we can do instead, I reasoned, was help our fellow creatures who were also created by Him — and in particular those burdened with unfortunate handicaps.

So I decided that I would try and establish a home for handicapped children. At that time, Subud members in Britain had gotten together to set up such a home. However, there was as yet no formal structure for welfare projects within Subud. Nowadays, many Subud members are actively engaged in welfare schemes, under the umbrella of the Susila Dharma International Association, whose humanitarian activities are highly regarded by the UN. However, at that time Subud members were still learning how to run their own Subud groups and latihan activities.

This was also the situation in Japan and my goal to establish a home for the handicapped did not receive much support at the time. Unfortunately, I had absolutely no funds or experience, but as I continued my efforts, two members emerged to offer their help. One was a paediatrician who told me he owned a plot of land in his home town along the coast, which he offered as somewhere to build a home for handicapped children. To me, who had been thinking that at least if we had the land we could do something, this was an unexpected godsend.

However, when the three of us were ready to visit the land, an obstacle emerged. After the doctor had contacted relatives from his home town, the response came that since he had left the management of the land to them for so many years, while he might still be the owner in name, he could not dispose of the land in any way he wished. They were also strongly prejudiced against the handicapped and told him that nobody would agree to the use of the land for such a purpose. So the project had to be shelved.

After that, nothing emerged to help realise this goal, but I was determined not to give up. At least, my role in Subud had been fulfilled — my desire to have the latihan take root in Japan had been granted, and Subud had been re-established with a new structure and new conditions. My responsibility had now ended, so I thought. What needed to follow therefore was for me to put everything I had into pursuing what had been revealed to me as the purpose of my soul, and one way to do that was still to set up welfare projects. Looking at it that way, the Subud group seemed limited and dull; it was a tiny organization with no social powers. To me, it was just like a group of friends dealing with each other's problems. I wanted more action — to be among people involved with social welfare, and working directly with them. However, hardly anyone else in the group shared my thoughts and I felt forced to pursue my goal separately from the Subud group.

SUBUD – A SPIRITUAL JOURNEY

It was that split-second experience I had had while interpreting Bapak's talk at the Subud World Congress in Tokyo that changed my ideas. Whilst I had from past experiences understood about Bapak's spiritual magnitude, the notion that he had been sent as God's 'agent', or that he represented something of God's power in this world was a new and astonishing revelation to me. What came to me then was how Bapak, as one of God's representatives on earth, might be able to do anything if he so wished, yet now here he was - investing all his time and energy to foster this tiny, valueless organization with no influence or social recognition. Bapak said that while the latihan, which was the working of God's power, could not be organized by human beings, we needed at the very least a worldly organization to go alongside it, so that Subud could gradually be spread throughout society. If Bapak thought that this was a priority and gave it his undivided attention, was it not the job of someone who wanted to serve God, to help Bapak in this work as far as was possible? It seemed to me that this was the ultimate I could give at that time.

It was a turning point for me. My life from then on became inextricably linked with the progress of the Subud Association. Whilst I did not abandon the dream of a welfare project, I changed the order of priority as regards my activity goals.

Tests by Bapak

I have mentioned before that testing is a type of latihan whereby one can seek guidance from the Almighty about problems that one cannot solve by oneself. As part of my descriptions of Bapak, I would like to write about some of the testing that he undertook with us members, in particular those that made a lasting impression on me and are still fresh in my memory.

Bapak undertook world trips many times. Sometimes, those trips would take over a year, as he visited many countries and many cities. During those trips, he would give talks, and carry out latihans and testing for the members. Any of these events was like a special bonus for members and of these, testing in particular was eagerly awaited by everyone. This was because these tests were ones that only Bapak could give.

Testing also has another purpose: by this method one can check how much progress one has made in one's latihan. Most of the tests Bapak carried out were for this purpose.

One of those tests that can also be experienced by newer members, checks which parts of one's body have been penetrated by the latihan. This is generally called 'body testing.' As I mentioned earlier, normally the effects of the latihan are initially felt through bodily movements and actions. When one begins the latihan, the hands and feet move independently of one's own will so that one may walk, run, sing, or dance. These are movements that come from the newly awakened soul in contact with the Power of God, and they serve to help purify the body.

Physical purification next progresses to purification of the senses, of the emotions and desires, of the will, and of one's thoughts. This is so that all the human functions can eventually become tools of God's power – but now through the soul, rather than as tools of one's own will and desires. Body testing is a first step to being able to check which parts of one's body have become purified so that they move in obedience to the commands of the soul.

Body testing consists of questions such as, 'Where are your hands? What are they used for?' And starting with the hands and feet, it then moves on to all parts of the body, external and internal. One listens to the questions in a latihan state, and sees how one's body responds to them. (Needless to say, it is no good moving from the will.) This allows one to understand and feel the difference between moving from one's own will and being moved by the Power of God.

After one has been doing latihan for some time, the body will move automatically in response to more complex questions. These could be questions such as, 'How does your body move when you dance like a Javanese?' or 'How does your body move when you are doing an Egyptian dance?' In response, the entire body will express dances from these places despite never having learned or practiced them. As progress in the latihan grows, members find that in response to questions about their inner lives, they will also have responses that are more internal. And ultimately, they will be able to respond from the level of their understanding and consciousness. These latter responses require a very advanced level of purification however, and for me this is still only a future possibility.

In this way, the tests that Bapak did with members would start with simple questions and then progress to deeper, more complex ones. Anything could become the subject of testing for us — even phenomena that went beyond this world. Some questions were relatively simple while others were subjects one had never consciously thought about. Once I was asked, 'How does a dog laugh?' According to my understanding, only humans can laugh - animals cannot. But through my response to that test, I became aware that dogs do laugh and humans can only hear this as barking.

Such a question was merely the beginning; some of the questions Bapak asked had a significance that I simply could not understand. When asked questions about the angels or ancient prophets, I would wonder again who was this person Bapak who enabled ordinary people like us to receive about such things for ourselves. Sometimes I received no responses. I think that Bapak would add these high-level questions into the mix to see if there was anyone who could receive answers to them and also to make us aware of the enormous potential of the latihan.

In some respect, it appeared that our ability to respond was dependent on the power and wherewithal bestowed on us by Bapak at the time. Where normally we did not possess the inner capacity to receive an answer to a question, Bapak's invisible boost allowed us to transcend our limitations a little and receive a response. This became clear if I tried to repeat a test by myself that I had experienced in front of Bapak. Despite the fact that the question was the same, I would be incapable of receiving or feeling anything.

When asked by members why they could receive better in his presence, Bapak replied that it is simply because Bapak's inner is more quiet. When we do latihan or testing together, our inners are somewhat linked, so that we help each other while we are not aware of it.

As I said before, it is difficult to explain the working of the latihan by words, and it will be even more difficult to understand the 'testing' for those who have not yet experienced it. Therefore, it is no wonder that people are suspicious that Bapak was using a sort of hypnotism in conducting testing with members. In fact, in the early days I received these questions even from Subud members, if they had not yet fully experienced the working of latihan.

The mechanism of hypnotism is not yet fully explained by science, but it is a technique to manipulate the mind and heart, by making use of their susceptibility to suggestion. The suggestion comes from the hypnotist and from his strong will expressed in words. And those who are hypnotized are more or less surrendering themselves to him. In short, it is a technique to control human behavior from outside and as such, it is completely different from the latihan or testing, in which we only submit to the power of God and shut off all the influences from outside, paying no attention to other people, including Bapak.

Once Bapak had died, there was no-one who could carry out these high-level tests with members and help them receive answers. For members doing the latihan now, since Bapak has died all they can do is continue their own process of purification until there comes a time when they can receive answers to these complex questions by themselves.

Before I finish this topic, I want to describe two high-level tests that Bapak did, whereby through his help I was able to have a receiving that bordered on the miraculous. For me, the result was nothing short of astonishing and made a lasting impression on me.

The first one was about the existence of life on the planet Jupiter and was one that Bapak tested with the members when he visited Japan. Questions about heavenly bodies other than Earth were quite rare amongst Bapak's tests. This was probably because Bapak knew that we were still incapable of receiving correct responses about anything beyond this world. Bapak acknowledged the existence of inhabitants on planets other than Earth, but he never referred to them as human beings, just as the 'beings' on these planets. According to Bapak, and as astronomers also have now confirmed, the environment on each of the planets is very different, and it followed that the conditions for the inhabitants was also different. He explained that human beings were incapable of physical exchange with these beings, and could only experience contact with them on a spiritual level.

When Bapak came to Japan in 1959, debate about UFO's was much more popular than it is now, and one of the members asked Bapak was it true what people had said about Venusians visiting Earth. The question had nothing to do with Subud or with the latihan and was one of personal interest, but Bapak answered it briefly saying, *'If beings from Venus came to Earth, the Earth would burn up.'* This was ten years before the Venus probe had succeeded in making a soft landing on the planet and verified that its surface was a scorching 470° heat.

At the time of these tests, it was my job to translate Bapak's questions and comments into Japanese, and so I was seated beside the English interpreter who was sitting next to Bapak. This meant that unfortunately, I was unable to join the other members to receive the tests and so I was resigned to simply concentrating on the translating. The group was divided into several smaller groups who would line up in turn before Bapak in a latihan state to receive the test. Bapak would then ask a question in Indonesian; this would be interpreted into English, and then I would translate it into Japanese. Once they heard my Japanese and understood the question, the members would be moved from within and receive an answer to the test. In this way, they could find out for themselves just how far they had progressed in their latihan, instead of being told by someone else.

And then, out of the blue, Bapak suddenly asked a completely unrelated question.

"What kind of heart do the beings on Jupiter possess?"

As I mentioned earlier, this kind of question was very rare for Bapak to ask and to miss receiving this meant that one would probably never have the opportunity to test it again. And so, once I had interpreted the question into Japanese, I hurriedly shut my eyes and tried to receive something, no matter how little it might be.

In a flash, a silvery, hazy mist spilled out from my chest like a breath and sparkling brightly, scattered and spread till it was several meters in front of me. I heard Bapak's voice say, "Stop!" and I quickly returned to my interpreting role. Bapak asked the members, "did you receive anything?" and an American who had joined in the testing put up his hand.

"It felt light," he said.

"Yes, bright!" said Bapak in English.

With these words, I realized that the content of what I had received was not mistaken. The beings on Jupiter were spiritually advanced and possessed hearts of such purity that they were incomparable to human beings. That is what I experienced.

A further experience I had was during a test that took place in Bapak's house in Indonesia. I had come as a helper representative from Japan along with a committee member to take part in the Subud Asian Zone Meeting.

One of the items on the agenda was the first Compact Council (a Council made of representatives from each Zone) that was to take place in England the following year. We had to decide which country from Asia would take part as the representative of the Asian zone, and at the meeting, it was decided that this should be Indonesia.

However, when this was reported to Bapak the following day, he uncharacteristically expressed his disapproval and said,

"If you would allow me to suggest it, I would like to put forward Japan."

These unexpected words from Bapak threw the Indonesian representatives into confusion as well as us, the Japanese representatives.

Bapak spoke with the Indonesian representatives for a little while and then as if he had gained consent, turned to me and asked,

"Can you travel to the UK?"

Dismayed by this sudden turn of events, I replied,

"I do not have the capacity nor do I think I am qualified to be a representative."

In fact, I wanted to refuse. As a salaried worker, it was hard for me to take a lengthy holiday every year, and I did not feel I was sufficiently good at English to be able to take part in group discussions with the other Zone reps from around the world. I was not confident for these and other reasons.

But in response, Bapak said,

"It is not you that does the work; it is the Power of God that does the work."

These unexpected words from Bapak took me by surprise and I simply could not think of an excuse that would allow me to refuse.

Bapak then told me to test in front of the members. Bapak's first instructions to me were to walk like I normally do and then to walk in a state of latihan. This was a test that was familiar to me. I closed my eyes, went into a latihan state and started to walk. When I reached a wall, my legs would automatically do a U-turn so that I did not bump into it. Then Bapak instructed me to sit down to receive the next test.

He said, "I will say *Allah* using my heart and mind and then I will say *Allah* in a latihan state. Feel the difference between the two."

He rose from his chair. As I have mentioned before, a latihan state is one in which one is accompanied by the power of God. I closed my eyes and turned my attention and consciousness inwards.

"*Allah!*" I could hear Bapak's voice. A feeling of joy and lightness spread in my chest. If this were the feeling when Bapak said "*Allah!*" using his heart and mind, how amazing it would be when he called on the name of God in a latihan state. This was my thought as I waited for the next test.

"*Allah!*" I heard Bapak's voice. The tone of his voice and its expression hardly differed from the previous one, but then something happened which I could never have imagined.

I was in the midst of a terrifying silence. Doubtless, 'terrifying' is not a suitable adjective, but it can only be described by words such as terrifying or frightful. There was none of the joy that I had anticipated. On the contrary, all human emotion and feelings had been entirely wiped out. What I was feeling was the silence of a ruin. It felt as though the world had come to an end and all living things were extinct. There was no sound and I was the only person surviving, standing alone in the emptiness. This was a bottomless pit of silence that was fundamentally different to the silence I had experienced in my latihans. I was so frightened; it felt as though the hairs on my body were standing on end.

When the test ended, Bapak asked, "did you feel the difference?"

My experience had been so shocking that words failed me – I could only nod. Bapak smiled.

The test changed my concept of God. I still do not fully understand what I actually experienced then but it did remind me of Bapak's words:

"God existed before everything was created and God will exist after everything has ended."

It is quite possible that in this way, I was given a glimpse of the essence of the Supreme Being which will exist after everything has ended. Of course, I cannot be sure but it was an experience that I will never forget. I do know that at the very least this was the doorway to a silence that was incredibly more profound and vaster than the inner silence I experience in latihan.

The following year, I did go to England as Bapak had suggested and began my activities in Subud on an international level.

SUBUD – A SPIRITUAL JOURNEY

Testing and the outer life

I will add one more story about testing which related more to my outer life and my material condition, although it was not one of Bapak's tests. It happened 5 years before the preceding story and it was not I who tested this time but my wife, and she did it in a dream!

One night in late 1970 she shook me awake, saying "I have just had a strange dream. It had no story or plot. I was just told to test. So I tested how our material condition would become in the future, and I received that it would become much much better than now. Then I tested how we ourselves would develop spiritually in the future and received that this also would become better. Then I woke up."

I could not take it seriously, and said jokingly "why didn't you put the second question first?" Then I fell asleep again because it was still only the middle of the night.

My wife repeated the same story next morning, but even then I paid no attention to what she appeared to have received in the dream. First of all, it was out of the question to imagine that my income might soon increase considerably. After all, I was just an ordinary employee. Based on the Japanese lifetime employment and seniority system, my salary might increase every year, but by only a few percent. It would take not 10 but 20 years for my income to be doubled.

Also, a patent firm is similar to a law firm, and so is the office of patent attorneys. Other staff are all their assistants or clerks, as it were. The patent office I worked with was one of the biggest patent firms in Japan as well as in the world; it had more than 200 members, including 30 patent attorneys, who were naturally treated better than others. The office was managed by the director and eight department managers who were all senior patent attorneys, with only one exception. This man was not a patent attorney but had helped the director from the time when the firm began. Therefore, the future of any other unqualified staff was very limited. So I just ignored what my wife told me, and forgot about it completely.

As a matter of fact, I had a more serious worry on my mind at that time and I could not solve it until 1971. It was about my participation in the 4th Subud World Congress which was scheduled for August, 1971.

This Congress was somewhat special compared to other Congresses. It was the first World Congress being held in Bapak's home country, and it was the first Subud Congress to take place on its own premises. These were now being completed as the first Subud International Center, and were in a suburb of Jakarta. Moreover, it was considered to be a good opportunity to officially announce Subud's international character to the general public in Indonesia and to the Indonesian government. For this reason, the length of the Congress was to be not just the usual 10 days, but was set to be for one month, and it was planned that President Suharto and his wife should be invited to the opening ceremony, and that he should be asked to make an opening speech.

The problem with me was whether I could have permission from my firm for one month's leave in order to attend this Congress. My common sense was clearly saying 'No' to this question. The Japanese are known as workaholics. Although Japanese society has greatly changed in the last 30 to 40 years, in the early 1970s, it was still difficult for any company employee to have even 7 successive days off, for reasons other than illness.

The situation was the same with my firm and there had been no precedent for holidays of more than one week. So it was customary in those days and with my firm that if someone wanted to travel abroad for sightseeing, for instance, they just resigned from the firm.

"I will probably have to quit the firm", I thought, but I was indecisive. It seemed clear that what I should do was talk with the director about my wish, and if it was refused, then decide whether to leave the firm or give up the Congress. However, I did not have the courage to talk to him right away, so I postponed it day after day.

Then in February, the director called me to his room one afternoon. He said he was planning to reorganize the department that I belonged to and would like to appoint me as the manager of the foreign application department that was to be formed. His words were quite unexpected and surprising, but I quickly made up my mind and said.

"I am grateful as to your intention, but I wish to decline this appointment."

I explained that I belonged to a certain spiritual movement and it was organizing a World Congress in August, and that this World Congress had a special importance for me and I was thinking of participating in it. But in order to do so, I would need an exceptionally long leave from the office.

And I continued, "I know that it is contrary to the longstanding practice of this firm for employees to give long periods of leave for private purposes. I also understand that the department manager should be able to give an example toward other department members as to his behaviour. So I am afraid that if I become a department manager, my action may have an undesirable effect on the firm. Actually, I have been thinking of leaving the firm."

It was apparent that the director had taken it for granted that I would be delighted with this appointment, and in fact, it was a very unusual promotion for an unqualified employee like me. The director got a little confused and said, "if that is the case, let me think over the matter again, for a while."

One week later, he again called me to his room and said, "I weighed up the pros and cons for my firm, and came to the conclusion that it is better for us to keep you rather than lose you, even though you will be taking one month's leave. I know that you are respected by your colleagues."

Thus it was that in April I was appointed the manager of the foreign application department. My income then more than doubled, just as had been foretold by my wife. And I could attend the 4th Subud World Congress for the whole time, together with my wife.

Religion and the Latihan

While Subud does have relevance to religion in that it is a pathway to God, it is not of itself a religion nor is it connected to any particular religion. Religions always have doctrines but Subud has no doctrine and no theory. Doctrines and theories are learnt through the mind; the latihan cannot be learned, or understood by the brain or executed by one's will. Bapak repeatedly insists that the latihan is only to be received. The latihan can only be experienced and it is through this that understanding is born and people learn. That is why it can be said to be extremely practical.

Such being the case, we may say that Subud is a form of education, but not from the human mind. It is not an education and learning based on some theory, but is the learning from within and from our own soul, which comes in touch with the power of the Supreme Being who created us human beings as well as the whole universe.

It is a fact that Subud members do include those who belong to a religion and also those who have no particular religion. Amongst Subud members are Christians, Buddhists, Muslims, Jews, Hindus and those from other faiths, and even people who don't believe in religion at all. People have no difficulty in practising their religions whilst also practising the latihan. Indeed Bapak recommended this, because the latihan allows us to experience on a spiritual level the universal truths that lie deep within all religions, giving us an even better understanding of them. Some religions incorporate teachings and standards that are not actually based on spiritual truths, but through the latihan, believers can become aware of those teachings that are authentic and those that are not.

The latihan of Subud and its relevance to religion is a topic that can probably be debated from many angles. I am not going to engage with those issues at this point, but will talk instead about how the experiences I had in my own Subud life transformed my own attitude towards religion and my understanding of it.

While the religion of my family was Zen Buddhism, my upbringing was strongly influenced by the Seicho-no-Ie religion and when I first encountered Subud and started doing latihan, my job was editor of a journal from a publishing company that was a subsidiary organization of Seicho-no-Ie. My religion therefore, was based on the teachings of Dr. Taniguchi of Seicho-no-Ie.

And then, about one year after I had started the latihan, I kept having a recurring dream. It was a dream about shoes.

When the latihan begins to penetrate a man's inner, quite a few people talk about experiencing more significant dreams than ever before. This is because the transformations that occur inside as an effect of the latihan are sometimes manifested as dreams. It was around that time also that I experienced my first dream in brilliant technicolour. Many of my dreams concerned water, for example, dreams about being overwhelmed by floods and big waves. I did not understand their meaning, but since it is said that water is connected to one's emotions, these might have been about my own emotions. Whatever the case, these dreams had zero connection to my everyday life, and so I supposed that they could have been expressions of the transformation going on inside me, as a result of the latihan.

However, the dream I had about shoes was somewhat different from these other dreams. This one constantly repeated itself as though it was trying to tell me something. While the scenery in the dream would change, the story was always the same. I would be somewhere and about to go home, when I would not be able to find my shoes. No matter how hard I searched, I could not find them and so I could not go out. Sometimes it would be raining, or the road would be too muddy to walk barefoot; and then I would wake up in the middle of looking for my shoes.

I had that recurring dream over several months and it became really disturbing, but I simply could not understand the reason for it. Nor would it quite fit any Freudian Dream Theory. One day, however, the meaning came to me intuitively. I was sitting at my desk when the thought came to me that maybe the shoes symbolized religion for me; this insight allowed me to perceive the true form of my connection with my religion. This in turn was related to what I was seeking to gain from religion, and why I felt I needed to have one.

Shoes are a means to protect the feet. Our feet are what connect us to the earth. We wear shoes to protect our feet from getting hurt by stones or from getting dirty, but it is through this protective material, that we avoid direct contact with the earth. In the same way, it seemed, religion was a type of protection that kept me from getting injured when I came into direct contact with the world.

As an ethical framework, religion (and this includes theories and ideologies) provides us with a means to understand what happens in the world, acting as a ready-made way to interpret what we encounter in society. This also tells us what is wrong and what is right and how to understand the events that face us, so that we will not be hurt or bewildered by them. Moreover, the reality of the world always contains something unknown, and is filled with dangers that are unexpected (think how it is for babies and infants). But religion can be a kind of protection between the world and ourselves, just as shoes protect our feet so that we do not have to come into direct contact with the earth.

Through religion, the world is transformed into something comprehensible, something we can now safely incorporate into our own beliefs. In other words, if we have a religion or an ideology, we are able to interpret safely whatever reality we encounter, while still maintaining the integrity of our minds and hearts. This was for me, the real role of religion. I used to be extremely fearful of the world – afraid of becoming confused and wounded by any direct contact with it. So I used religion as a means of protection to prevent this from happening.

The dream in which I could not find my shoes and was hesitant about going outside, was surely telling me to have the courage to walk barefoot on the earth. Surely, this was about dropping my preconceptions, and seeing the world as through the eyes of a child, accepting things and people just as they are. And this would allow me to follow the guidance from within, and act in accordance with it. That was how I saw it.

This was a rather high ideal - similar to that which Confucius described when he said, *'At seventy, I became able to follow whatever my heart desired without transgressing from what was right.'* I knew this was the direction I had to take in future, now that I had received the inner compass of the latihan. Up till then I had been convinced that I did not need religion. I was happy with the latihan, which seemed to fulfil all my religious needs.

Once I had that thought, the shoes dreams ceased. This state of mind continued for over ten years. Moreover, it seemed to me that to be non-religious had become the norm in Japan, where recently religions had crystallised and lost their vitality.

Nevertheless, Bapak's advice had been not to ditch one's religion when one joined Subud. While Bapak himself was born a Muslim and continued to practice Islam until the end of his life, he never once made a value judgement about any religion or attempted to lure people to Islam. He told members seeking a new religion that they should choose one that suited the nature of their own soul. But I did not fully comprehend the significance of this and thought that the latihan was quite sufficient for me.

Then, ten years later, something happened that was to transform my opinion about religion. One day, I was chatting to a French-speaking Canadian member as we headed along a main street towards a station, weaving our way through the crowds. Mostly, it was my companion who was talking while I listened. His talk turned to circumcision - a practice that is common to both Judaism and Islam. I cannot remember what he said, but while I listened I happened to glance at my chest, whereupon what I saw made me doubt my own eyes. I was walking along stark naked through a large crowd of people. Of course, objectively speaking, this was a split-second illusion, but to me at the time it felt as though I really was walking naked along the road. Although this was just an image of myself, as usual, it brought with it a powerful sense of reality along with an intuition as to what the experience signified.

The naked body that I had seen was an expression of the inner me. After many years of latihan, the inner me was continually growing and being reborn; but there was no outer self to match the newly-acquired spiritual self. That was why I was naked. And the outer covering that this invisible self had to take on for this world was religion. Babies are born naked but to live in this world, humans need to be clothed. To be without clothes is not customary human behaviour. Clothing should also suit the wearer as it is partly the outward expression of that person's inner characteristics. So even if I thought the latihan was all I needed, without a religion I would lack an outer counterpart to match my inner content; I would not be complete as a human being in this world if I had no religion.

The understanding came to me in an instant, and so I chose Islam. Even though this was long before the emergence of fundamentalist Islamic terrorists, there was still a lot of resistance to conversion to the Islamic religion. Of the world's religions, Islam is the least familiar to the Japanese who consider it to be a strange, polygamous belief. I also had some personal resistance to circumcision. In spite of this, I converted to Islam because it seemed closest to what I had experienced when I first started out on my search for God. Monotheism seemed much closer to my inner nature than polytheism, as did Islam's emphasis on the omnipotence, transcendence, and greatness of Allah as creator and ruler of the universe and on His love for the human beings He created. Of the other monotheistic religions, Islam seemed to take the most purified form with its advocacy of absolute devotion and submission to Allah. This simplicity and purity was closer to my inner feelings than any other religion. Moreover, Islam is not coloured with the exclusivity of some other religions or cultures, and its belief that God sent not just Muhammad but many prophets from all races as his apostles, is testimony to Islam's universality and tolerance towards other religions.

To be honest however, I am by no means a model Muslim. Apart from doing the Ramadan fast, I do not obey many of the precepts. Despite this, I did have several experiences that were relevant to Islam. For example, during my first Ramadan fast, I discovered that Ramadan has a deeper spiritual significance than simply fasting from food, and on the evening of the first day, I returned from work to find that though there were no flowers about, the house was filled with a sweet fragrance.

The Koran also talks about the final ten nights of Ramadan as the 'Nights of Power,' when the gates of Heaven open and the angels and the Holy Spirit are sent to earth. While it may not have been that exact experience, on the 21st night, I felt something that was close to this description.

I was awake until nearly three o'clock in the morning that night, and had a headache. However, at the same time I started to feel a kind of luminosity within my chest. As time passed, the headache got worse but the sensation of luminosity in my chest increased, until I became flooded with joy. It was strange that despite the bad headache I was so happy inside - as if the physical pain was totally irrelevant. Then I noticed something shining in the corner of the room. I tried to make out what it was, but could not see its shape. Its brightness lasted only a minute or two, and I thought it might have been an angel, but who can be sure?

I also had other unusual experiences when I read the Koran. For example, I was reading one chapter every night during Ramadan and one night, I finished reading it and shut the book. I put the Koran on my chest without intention and was surprised to find that without taking account of my clothes, it just entered straight into my chest. Of course it was just a feeling, but it seemed like a reality, because for a while I kept having a sense of the book's shape within my chest. I was not sure what this meant, but it may have indicated that I had absorbed the book's content into my being, so that it became one with me.

I mentioned earlier that the latihan allows us to feel on a spiritual level the reality that lies hidden behind the creeds and ceremonies of our religions, and I would like to describe another example of this.

The idea that Islam is an aggressive religion is one that has been spread through Western European society since the Crusades of the Middle Ages. The idea has been even more strengthened recently by Islamist terrorists claiming the legitimacy of *Jihad* (holy war) for their acts of terror and violence. Whilst the image of Muslims holding the Koran in one hand and a sword in the other is a mistaken one, it is true that Islam does have the concept of a holy war, and the expression, 'The Sword of Islam' does exist.

I converted to Islam, but my understanding of Islam was that it cherished peace and was tolerant towards other religions. The concepts of a sword or *Jihad* were therefore difficult for me to accept.

Once in the course of a conversation about something else, I recall Bapak telling us, *'Jihad is not a fight against people. It is a fight against the nafsu.'* The *nafsu* refers to the will and desires of human beings. To be honest, when Bapak said this, I only half understood what he meant by the difference between fighting people and fighting the *nafsu*. Although these were Bapak's words, I felt inadequate and simply not up to the task of interpreting them. The experience I am about to relate was connected to this.

On that day, I had joined in a group latihan. Halfway through, I started to get a sense that I was inside something. As the feeling became clearer, I was astonished to find that I was inside an enormous sword. It was a transparent sword with the tip pointing downwards and I was dancing and singing and doing my latihan inside it. I realized that this was the Sword of Islam (though it was not an Arabian curved sword but a double-edged sword) and it was the task of the sword to cut away my *nafsu*, so that I could continue my latihan easily and without interference from it. The *nafsu* are entwined with human consciousness and it is impossible for us to separate them by ourselves. The Sword of Islam was the Power of God, given to us so that we can cut away the *nafsu* that accompany our true selves. The experience taught me this and gave me an understanding of what Bapak meant when he talked about *Jihad* ('holy war').

I learned afterwards that orthodox Islamist scholars say that the original meaning of *Jihad* is 'to strive' and there is a problem with translating it to mean 'holy war.' Originally, *Jihad* chiefly meant the struggle against one's base desires and this is called a Greater *Jihad*, while the struggle against one's external enemies is called a Lesser *Jihad*. This latter is generally used only to mean a struggle that is in self-defence. The Koran defines it in this way:

'And fight in the way of Allah with those who fight with you, and do not exceed the limits, surely Allah does not love those who exceed the limits.'
(The Cow 2.190)

This can be interpreted to mean that it is against the teachings of Islam to carry out indiscriminate acts of violence against those who are unarmed, including of course, women and children.

I have so far written the experiences which relate to the religion of Islam that I embraced. However, my favorite holy book in my youth was the New Testament which recorded the life of Jesus Christ and his words and I could not help but admire the beauty of his words every time I read them. In short, Jesus was a special person for me and I deeply loved him and respected him with great sympathy. This is probably the reason why I was once given a precious experience about him.

Similarly to other times, this event happened without any warning. One afternoon, I was sitting alone in my room. I do not remember what I was going to do, but suddenly the atmosphere around me appeared to become very quiet, and the state of my inside also changed. In the next moment, I realized that I was experiencing the state of feeling that Jesus had in a particular situation. It was as if my inner became identical with that of Jesus and he was saying, 'Come and drink from me. This is the Water of Life from the well that will never dry up. And those who drink this water will never feel thirsty again.' Of course, his words as reported in the Bible are a little different, but I felt that a spiritual current was entering my inner feeling like a pure stream and I instinctively understood that it was what Jesus was feeling. This spiritual current was full of love and compassion. 'Oh, this is he, Jesus', I thought.

The experience lasted only a minute or so, but it had a deep impact on me. The feeling I experienced is inexplicable but I was sure I was made to understand what kind of person Jesus was, at least partly, and not through the written word, but as first hand knowledge. Since then, his existence has become even more special to me and I am grateful to the Almighty that I was given this experience.

On Death

Death is for us the ultimate riddle. If there is anything we can be 100% certain about, it is that at some point, we will die. But, we know nothing about death. Nobody has the answer to the questions: what is death, why do humans die, and what happens to us after we die.

People fear death more than anything else. There are two opposing opinions about it. Some people think that death is the end and do not believe that the soul continues to live after death. This thought is supported by science and is the mainstream belief of our times. It maintains that human psychological activity is the chemical effect of the workings of the brain and therefore when the brain is no more, nothing else survives. People who believe this take their comfort from the notion that we live on in the memories of our family and others. They also think that it is inevitable that the 'I' disappears completely, since we are made of matter and therefore must return to the material universe.

The opposing opinion is that the soul does continue to exist after physical death. This opinion is supported by traditional thought but in this case too, people cannot fully answer the question of what actually happens to someone after death. Even if there is supporting evidence in the form of ghosts, near-death experiences, and spiritual channelling, nobody has come back to life after they have died to testify as to the truth. And even, if we do believe in near-death experiences and channelling, there is no way of knowing just how true these stories are. We used to think that our entire universe was Earth until we discovered that the earth is no bigger than a poppy seed in our galaxy. In the same way, it is possible that the hereafter is infinitely vaster than the earth we live on.

In some way, the latihan brings us closer to our own death and to the spiritual world beyond. It can be said that the latihan state - where the workings of one's thoughts, desires, and emotions are stilled, is close to the state of death. The latihan awakens the soul – an entity which lives on after it crosses the threshold of death – and helps it to grow. It is possible that the latihan acts as a bridge that connects this world with the next. Bapak said that we would probably only understand the true significance of the latihan when we die.

In the course of practising the latihan, I have come to the conclusion that both conflicting opinions are right, and both are wrong. In other words, it depends on the state of the person's soul. Some people may die and that may be the end of them; the soul of others may continue to exist after their death; and yet other souls may continue to grow through transmigration.

Bapak often referred to the life after death in his talks, but I do not remember any definite and detailed explanation that he gave on this subject. However, in the book *A Memoir of Subud*, written by Varindra Tarzie Vittachi after Bapak's death, I did find an interesting quote from a conversation Varindra had with Bapak during which Varindra asked Bapak about life after death. I will take the liberty of quoting this here. (Varindra Vittachi was chair of the World Subud Council and the World Congresses for 26 years, and was also a world-famous journalist, a columnist for *NewsWeek* magazine, and someone who greatly helped the plight of poor children from around the world through his role as director of public relations at UNICEF.)

"After a while, Bapak [ ] said, 'You are not ready to receive and understand the full answer. But Bapak will tell you something you can understand. A temporary explanation. Bapak will speak in very broad terms and if you speak or write about it you should always point out that it is a broad explanation. An explanation for now, not the whole explanation. There are three broad categories of possibilities for human beings after death. The first and the largest category is people who are so completely influenced by the material forces of the earth that when they die, their jiwas (our inner content, soul) are so heavily encrusted with material forces that they revert to the material earth along with their bodies.'

I must have looked horrified at this prospect not only for them but for myself too – just in case – for Bapak immediately added, 'But there is always God's mercy. One of their progeny, within seven generations, may receive the grace of God and that person's worship would influence the soul of the earth-bound ancestor and enable it to begin progress to the origin.

'The second category is the people who have worshipped God as sincerely as they can. They attend the mosque and church, regularly perform their shariat (religious rite) and are referred to as "God fearing" men and women. Their jiwas may not be as heavily encrusted by the material forces and when they die, their jiwas do not revert to earth but hover about on its surface. These are what people often see as "ghosts". They have two possibilities of redeeming themselves. One of their progeny within seven generations may come in contact with the Grace of God and this will touch them and set them off on their way to the true human world. The second possibility is rebirth. If a man and woman in a state of being

similar to that of the dead person while he was on earth, are entering into a procreative act, the 'hoverer' could enter the crucible of that union and become the soul of the child who may be born from it. That child might come into contact with the grace of God in its lifetime and, at death, will begin the journey to the true human world.

'The third category is the smallest and includes Subud members who have received the contact with the power of God. Depending on the sincerity of this person's surrender and the degree of purification reached in his or her lifetime, their soul, when separated from the body, will soon be on its ascendance to the true human world. It will not remain in earth's atmosphere but will go beyond this solar system, making its way eventually to the origin.' Bapak stopped, and feeling the solemnness his explanation had caused in Usman and me, he cracked a joke: 'No guarantees!' And then, he repeated his warning that he was 'speaking broadly' and that this was only a partial explanation."

I am not qualified to make a comment, but I did have some experiences that proved to me that there is no rule about death and it depends on the individual case. In particular, there were three experiences that I would like to mention. The first one was about a year after I had started to do the latihan, when I was still a long way from having true spiritual experiences. It came in the form of a dream. Unlike other dreams, this one was unusual in that it was structured like a serial story about circumstances that suggested a certain type of death.

The third experience I will describe is in complete contrast to the first.

1. Death of a Friend

I heard about the death of Shoichi just after I had got married. Shoichi had been to primary and junior high school with me and lived close by. He had been one of my good friends until we had to leave after the war, and I had no opportunity to meet him again. I was later shocked to hear from a friend that while he was with his mother he had killed himself by leaping in front of a train at a railway crossing. I felt a sense of great regret; regret because not long before another friend had told me that Shoichi had recently become interested in Indian philosophy, and had expressed a desire to meet me. However, I had just started my newly married life and had put off contacting Shoichi until later. He had been an only child of a single mother who had doted and depended on him, and so it felt like his death was even more painful for her. That was when I had the first dream.

In the dream, I was walking with Shoichi through pitch darkness. It felt like we were on a path that went through a park, but it was too dark to see anything. I could not even see his shoulder or his face as he walked beside me, to my left. I could just feel his presence and that is how I knew he was there.

I was talking to him because I wanted him to know about the existence of God. However, it was clear that he was not yet ready to accept any talk of God, and so I could not use the word 'God.' I was forced to start with something less challenging that he might be able to accept. I said that more things existed in this world than could be seen by our ordinary eyes. Just like the wind, or electricity, there were things that were invisible but that still existed. In the same way, I eagerly explained, could it not be possible that there was a subtle, spiritual reality - another world that existed behind this one?

The dream ended with me passionately continuing to talk to him while walking this winding path in complete darkness.

One or two weeks later, I had another dream. This time, I was sitting at my desk in the editing department at the office where I worked. The room was arranged as normal. A door opened from a room just opposite and a man came in. I glanced up and was surprised to see that it was Shoichi, who should have been dead. *'Uh oh!'* I thought, and hurried to see if he was casting a shadow. If he had no shadow, I was thinking, everyone would know he was dead and the office would erupt in chaos. But I could not check whether he had a shadow or not because the desk was blocking my view. I hurriedly stood up, rushed to the door and pushed Shoichi out, guiding him somehow down the stairs and through the front hall, and from there to the outside.

We crossed a wide path and climbed a slope that led onto another big road. I tried to pull him across, but he suddenly leant right onto me, saying his leg was injured and he couldn't walk. I supported the weight of his body with my shoulder and reassured him saying,

"You're dead! You're dead and so there's no way your leg could hurt or that you could have a problem with it! Once you're dead, you don't get injuries so you should be able to walk, ok? All you have to do is say to yourself over and over 'I'm dead, I'm already dead' and then you should be able to walk."

The dream ended when I was still trying to haul his heavy body up the slope and trying to persuade him to walk.

Then, around two weeks later, I had another dream. This time, the scene was completely different and much more vivid. I had put several magazines like those from Seicho-no-Ie into a bag, and was about to visit Shoichi's NEW house. Though small, his two-storey house was neat. He greeted me amicably in the living room.

We chatted for a while until I had a thought. Shoichi's manner towards me seemed so natural that I started to doubt whether the Shoichi in front of me was actually dead and whether I had made a mistake. I became more and more concerned, thinking that if he were really alive after all, my behaviour had been very offensive. So then I came up with an idea to check if he really were dead or not. We were both seated on cushions on the *tatami* rush-mat. I decided I would get close to him and touch him. If he were dead, there would be no contact and I would just go through him.

So, while remaining seated, I started to edge towards him and casually, while we continued to converse, I lightly touched his knee with my knee. Unexpectedly, I came into contact with warm, living flesh. I felt frustration: so he was not dead after all! But that could not be the case either. Trying not to be noticed by him, I quietened my mind as for latihan and tried to feel my inner self. (This was the same state as when we do testing, but I did not know that.) Then I knew that there was no question - he really was dead. Of course, he was dead. I felt relief inside.

Then I noticed that Shoichi had fewer moles on his face. When we were children, there were so many clustered at the back of his neck that they formed a darker area. The moles had increased as he grew, and the last time I saw him, there had been too many to count, all over his face. But now the moles had decreased by about one third. So I said to him, "Oh, it's great that your moles have nearly gone!" He grinned shyly in response. I gave him the magazines I had brought and the dream ended with me leaving the house.

This was the last dream I had about Shoichi and he never appeared in my dreams again. But it was interesting that I heard several months later that when he had jumped in front of the train, he had broken one of his legs before he died.

I had the thought that probably the dreams had been a result of my soul coming into contact with the soul of my friend, without my being conscious of it. Of course, I could not be sure, but the thought helped to lessen the guilt I had felt about not contacting him while he was still alive.

2. The Realm of Death

That first experience and the dreams I had at that time, suggest there are cases when it is possible that the person who has died is not aware that they have died; when their consciousness stays fixed at the point of death and they exist in a state where time has stopped at that moment.

Of course, this is personal conjecture. Who knows what the after-life is really like – but the next experience I am going to describe gave me a small taste of the nature of that realm. And, as I mentioned earlier, nothing can be corroborated as no-one has come back from the dead to give us a report.

This is about an experience I had while I was doing latihan with a helper I was close to, several days before he died. I had visited his house to do a latihan beside him. He lay in bed to do the latihan and it seemed that he went to sleep half way through.

The latihan was very strong right from the beginning, and I could gradually feel myself sinking deeper and deeper into my inner self until it felt like I had reached the ocean floor. Stillness dominated the scene. I started to proceed slowly forwards as though through the ocean. After a while, I had to stop and felt that if I went any further I would not be able to retrace my steps. It felt like I had come close to the borderline between life and death. It was a strange feeling: I became aware that I had to stand there and could neither move forwards nor backwards. Maybe

I had come too close to the border of the domain of death, so that when I tried to walk I couldn't and when I tried to retreat, I couldn't. Worse, it felt like I could not even move my arms.

I became a little frightened, and tried to pray so that I could ask God for help. But, even more frighteningly, I could not pray. I wanted to pray but even the capacity of directing my feelings toward God simply deserted me. I started to get really scared. It felt like I would be stuck in that place for eternity. I understood the nature of the spiritual world that was ruled directly by God and I also understood about the next world, where it was not possible to move even a finger without the help of God's power. Unless God willed it, it was not even possible to get close to Him. I wondered if I had come too close to the domain of death and that if I could not go back, whether I would die in the place where I now found myself. Fortunately, I had been doing latihan and it was still working in me. So I was having that experience while still in a latihan state, and after a short while, I was able to return to normality.

The experience left a strong impression on me and also helped me to understand Bapak's words through experiencing them. Bapak had often told members not to believe what he himself said, but to experience it for themselves before they believed it. I had also heard Bapak say that when human beings die, their thoughts and emotions are immobilized, so that they cannot move or change or add to their content, and when asked by God about their behaviour in their lifetime, they cannot embellish or lie about it. By doing the latihan with a member who was close to death, it seems I was given the opportunity to experience, in a vicarious way, the actual state after death of having one's feelings immobilized and not being able to move.

3. A Departure Worthy of Celebration

The next story concerns the death of a friend, but it is completely different to the first experience about death that I have described. To a person whose soul has been awakened and experienced growth, death is not a sad event that should be mourned, but rather can become a joyful departure to a new life freed from the burdens of this world. I was able to confirm this. It was in fact a unique and unforgettable experience as I actually had a conversation with the deceased.

Haruhito was the helper I most trusted and he was my friend. He was younger than me and had been opened in Subud while he was a student at Kyoto University. He had assisted with the development of a Subud group in Kyoto and, after he graduated, with another one in Kyushu where he had gone to work. He had a job with a company which was under the umbrella of the biggest steel company in Japan, and in addition to being very good at his work, he was also very talented at handling people. He was sent on loan to the parent steel company in Tokyo several years later.

When he came to Tokyo, I was filled with optimism that we would be able to work together in close cooperation from then on. It was just around the time that a complex issue had emerged in my Subud group, and I felt that this could be resolved if we had him to help. However, he had not been in Tokyo very long before he was diagnosed with acute leukaemia and died soon after. This was an unbelievable event as he had been the picture of health until then.

Haruhito's death came as a shock and made a huge impact on me. Even now it seems strange, but I remember when I was told of his death over the phone, I felt as though my right arm had suddenly been amputated at the joint. It wasn't just that I had felt like this, it was actually the case that I could not feel my arm from the joint down. It was a very strange sensation. When I looked, I could see that my arm was still there, but it felt as though there was nothing from the joint down.

I have heard that amputees can still feel pain in their arms as though they were still attached, but I had never heard of an arm that was still attached feeling as though it suddenly did not exist. But I knew of the expression, *'to lose one's right arm'*, and it seems that it can literally feel like that too. It took about 20 to 30 minutes before the sensation of being alive came back into my arm. That was an indication of just how much of a shock his death was to me.

I attended the wake on the following night with my wife. When we got to his house, the room was already full of people and it was particularly crowded around the entrance. Since it looked like there was still space in front of the funeral altar,

I made my way through the crowd to get close to it, and sat down. The chanting of the Buddhist sutra had already begun and Haruhito's wife was sitting beside three small children, frequently wiping tears from her eyes.

I listened to the sutras being chanted and was looking at the photograph of Haruhito that had been placed in front, when I felt a brightness in my chest, and for some reason a feeling of happiness welled up in me. The feeling grew stronger as time passed until it seemed that the light that had filled my chest completely was now overflowing and lighting up the entire room.

At that moment, it seemed as though the face in the photograph was smiling at me, and the thought entered my mind that I would be able to speak to Haruhito now. I resolved not to question whether this was possible, but to give it a go anyway. There was something I wanted to say to Haruhito. I had not yet gotten over the shock of his death, and I felt like reproaching him for going off and dying like that ahead of me without a by-your-leave. So I just started straight off talking to him in my mind.

"Haruhito, you already know that I've got a very difficult problem on my hands. I was depending on your support for this. I don't have the confidence to deal with this problem without you here. What am I supposed to do about it?"

The answer came back in a flash. I heard it not as a voice but as words that just floated into my mind in the form of an answer.

"You don't have to worry. God will help you when it is needed."

That was a reply that was so like him. I pushed the point further.

"That's probably OK for you. In fact, you're probably quite happy but what about your wife and the kids that you've left behind? Your wife is crying and your children are still very young. Don't you think you were a bit selfish?"

His reply came after a moment's hesitation.

"I think God will look after them, you know."

I asked him a final question.

"What are you going to do now? Are you going to stay around here for a bit?"

By 'here,' I meant, not just in his house but in this earthly world.

"I don't know but I think I'm going to be told to go somewhere else pretty soon."

No other questions came into my mind. And so I left the conversation at that. However the brightness in my chest and the feeling of joy just got stronger and stronger until I felt I was going to start laughing out loud. Around me, many of the guests were mourning Haruhito's death as he had died so young and wiping tears away with their handkerchiefs, but I myself was in a state that was, strangely, the complete opposite. I had to struggle hard to compose my features so that I would not burst out laughing. Unlike the mourning of the family and relatives, I had witnessed a death that had, on the contrary, brought joy and happiness to the deceased. It was a departure that crossed the threshold of death but that shone with great brilliance – a brilliance that stayed within me until I had left his house.

Sincere Receiving

I wrote about how I was attracted to the simplicity and purity of the latihan of Subud when I first encountered it, and how I saw this as a sign of the direct workings of God. The meaning of 'purity' here is a state created by the latihan which is free from all the human elements such as the thoughts, emotions and the workings of the will, and all the other artificial props humans create to support themselves. This is because it is those that pollute the state of innocence with which we are born. Later we become accustomed to life in this world by sacrificing that state as we develop our thoughts and emotions; we then become adults by familiarizing ourselves with the knowledge of this world.

Therefore, when we start to do the latihan, we are neither pure nor innocent. Our inner selves are sullied not only by our appetites and blind ideas, but also by whatever deep-rooted weaknesses we have inherited from our parents and ancestors. Concealed within are also any warped tendencies inherent in our personalities and which Bapak characterised as being more serious than a major illness. Because of these many polluting elements, and because of being spurred on by every possible emotion, it is impossible to halt the workings of our mind, even in sleep.

The latihan reins in all these polluting elements, but it is not always the case that they can be quietened completely and immediately. They are quietened to the degree that will allow that person to come into contact with the power of God. As that person continues to practice the latihan, and as their purification progresses, the latihan of that person also increases in profundity, as they can then receive the latihan in a purer state.

Ibu Rahayu (Bapak's daughter) spoke about the process of purification thus in one of her talks:

"And receiving can progress even further, you can have a much purer receiving. This kind of receiving you have is an experience in which you feel that you have left this world. All you are aware of is yourself and the Power of God. This is what can be called true receiving. But this only happens if God wills it." (Ibu Rahayu's talk of 13 Aug 2003: Code No.03 SAO 3).

I was given an experience close to this description only once before. This happened in the mid-1980's, just before

Bapak died, while I was attending a World Subud Council meeting in Indonesia. On the day in question, latihan had been scheduled for 10.00 a.m. I had been suffering a slight headache and considered not attending latihan for that reason. However, since Bapak would also be present and my headache was not too overpowering, I decided to join in anyway. I waited in a place close to the exit for the latihan to begin, in case I had to leave early because of the headache. Bapak finally arrived and sat on the stage and the latihan began.

Not long into the latihan, I was less troubled by my headache. I then became aware that I was standing in a space that was void but for the power of God. The space spread out on all sides and was filled entirely with the power of God. Nothing else existed within that void except this, and as far as I could see, nothing moved. Everything was silent. God's power was just 'there', filling the space and I stood immobile myself.

Then, just as a gust of wind suddenly ripples the evening calm, there was a slight movement around me and then washing over me. And what was moving like wind was the Power of God. At that moment, my body started to sway as though in keeping with the flow of wind. My movements synchronized with that movement without the slightest deviation. They became like an elegant dance while tears flowed from my eyes and my heart was filled with gratitude. This was a true latihan. I danced at one with the Power of God. I felt that I was at the very origin of the latihan and experiencing that source. There was movement from the Power of God; that, in turn, moved me so that it was in fact, a creative act from that supreme Source.

Bapak had once said that the Power of God moving in the latihan is God's primal Force and is the same Force that created the universe. While I did not doubt that the latihan existed as the movement of God's will, the idea that this Force was the same one that God had used to create the universe was too vast for me to understand, and even though these were Bapak's words, I could not instantly believe them. However, once I had experienced that latihan, I knew first-hand that the latihan was a fresh creative act by the power of God. That experience helped me to believe Bapak's words. When the latihan ended, I found that I had somehow manoeuvred my way past plenty of people and ended up in the row directly in front of Bapak.

This experience was a kind of climax for me in my latihan practice. Reflecting on it later, it seemed that my headache had been a form of preparation for that latihan as willed by God, so that I would find it easier to put aside my thoughts. There is no doubt in my mind that I was able to experience this latihan because it took place in front of Bapak.

The World Congress in Colombia

Everyone who walks the Subud path has a different experience. That is because each of us is different, and the place of departure for our souls on this journey also differs from person to person. These differences determine the road we each need to walk and the experiences we need to have. As a result, some people have a journey that is relatively uneventful, while the lives of others are filled with incident and excitement.

The journey I embarked on with the latihan as my companion taught me what I was supposed to do. Thus it was, by the time I reached my mid-forties, that I found myself making a living in a patent firm and simultaneously being involved in Subud activities on an international level. I have experienced many events and difficulties since then, but as they are not within the scope of this book, I will leave them aside.

However, there is one experience I will mention. This occurred in 1993, at the 8th Subud World Congress that was held in Colombia in South America. The reason I want to mention this experience is because it was connected to one I had 30 years earlier in which I had been given an indication of the purpose of my soul.

Back in 1963, I had been shown that my soul's purpose was to become a humble servant of God, but since that time I had been given no more indications of that kind. The difficulty of actually achieving this goal became ever clearer as time went on. For example, the notion of total surrender is easy to talk about, but incredibly difficult to put into practice. This is because it requires a deep trust in God, and an inner strength, awareness, and control that does not get overwhelmed by one's thoughts and feelings. It is an issue that accompanies my whole life, and one that I have gradually learned about through various experiences and trials. Despite this, I am still far from being able to achieve this state towards any circumstances in which I might find myself. We may say that to become God's servant, which is indeed the 'supreme goal of the soul,' goes beyond the span of a lifetime in this world.

In 1993, I became Chair of the International Subud Committee (ISC). The ISC is the executive arm of the international World Subud Association (WSA). Subud holds a World Congress once every four years, and the location and Chair of the ISC office changes with each Congress. Japan hosted the ISC office from 1989, and it took a lot of courage and determination for me to declare my candidacy for ISC Chair.

Until then, the ISC had been hosted only by countries in the West; in the UK, the USA, Canada, Australia, and Germany. Subud Japan had many reasons to feel uneasy about taking on the executive tasks of the World Subud Association: there was the problem of language, that would be a major handicap to smooth communications amongst the different member countries, the problem of Japan's high prices and the costs of running an office there, and the need to employ staff with good English-speaking skills. There were hardly any English-speaking members in Subud Japan and my English skills were also not up to the mark. There was no doubt that we would need a native-English speaking secretary to help with the ISC work.

These problems were solved in a way that I could not have foreseen and that I saw as God coming to our rescue. An Englishwoman, Hermia Brockway, who till then had been living in Australia, spontaneously decided to come to Japan to help me as a secretary. The work of sorting and archiving the enormous number of writings and records of Bapak had become an important new role of the ISC, and again I was helped by an American archivist, Daniela Moneta who moved to Indonesia to sort out Bapak's papers and a Japanese woman helper skilled in English, Saodah Hayashi who took on the responsibility of archive coordinator. She became an international helper later. As far as costs were concerned, the ISC chair had to be a full-time job, but I gave up my salary because the WSA was desperate for funds at the time. I asked the patent firm where I was working to reduce my workdays, and gave up my Saturdays and holidays. This continued without a break for four years.

The reason for my accepting the work of ISC chair was that in 1987, Bapak had unexpectedly died. I had been an international helper at the time and when I thought about the future of Subud after Bapak's death, I felt that we needed to give it a more international face and form. Until then the international task within Subud had been carried on by Western countries for the sake of convenience, but it seemed to me that now it was time to change this and to create an example of a non-Western country taking on a job like the ISC.

One of the biggest challenges facing me was the preparation and holding of a World Congress, which was one of the duties of the ISC. There were many difficulties involved in Japan hosting such a large-scale world event and, eventually, after testing the question, it was decided that the 8th Subud World Congress would actually be held on the other side of the world from us, in Colombia, South America. As a result of this, Subud Colombia was entrusted with the task of preparing the on-site requirements of the venue such as a large conference hall and accommodation, while it was the job of the ISC to supervise the entire project.

This was all possible thanks to the zeal and concerted support of the Colombian members. However, to prepare and host a Congress where over 1,500 members from all over the world gathered in Colombia for two weeks was not without its challenges. In particular, this Congress had set itself a daunting task: an ambitious plan to construct a vast latihan hall with a capacity for over 1,500 people, on the piece of land the Colombian members had acquired, while keeping within their very limited budget. In the interests of staying as close as possible to that budget, Muchtar Martins, a genius architect from Portugal, had designed a totally unique timber-framed Great Hall, using local materials.

As the world's cocaine-producing capital, Colombia is notoriously dangerous thanks to the frequency of kidnappings by anti-government armed forces and the drug mafia. For this reason, the safety of the congress participants was an essential factor, and there were more than a few voices of dissent about the perils of holding the World Congress in Colombia. I visited Colombia twice before the Congress to meet with the local organizers and repeatedly had to make difficult decisions. A major issue was whether the latihan hall would be ready before the opening day. Muchtar Martins had built himself a small hut on site and had been living there for several months, so that he could supervise the construction directly. But when I arrived in Colombia, the latihan hall was still under construction and was not completed until the day before the opening of the Congress.

When opening day came, I had to carry out a final inspection before the first latihan, which was scheduled for 10.00 a.m. This meant I did not have time to sit and calm myself before the latihan started. When I set foot inside the hall at 10.00 o'clock, my mind was still full of the meeting I had just come from. I knew very well from experience that I would not be able to have a proper latihan if I started off with my mind in that state, and I regretted this as it should have been a latihan celebrating the opening of Congress. I was resigned to the fact that I would spend the greater part of the 30 minutes trying to empty my mind and thus finish up with a shallow, superficial latihan.

As soon as I began, however, the very opposite to what I had imagined occurred. I could clearly feel that God's Presence was close. It was as though God was there and looking down on me. In all my many years of experience, it was rare for me to actually feel this Divine Presence during a latihan. I had felt it before only at the World Congress in Canada, but then it had lasted only 20 to 30 seconds. This time, however, the feeling of this Presence lasted from the very beginning to the very end.

It was not that I had been given something special from God at that time; it was simply that I had felt this Supreme Presence. But the significance of it was not lost on me. It was to do with the fact that I had not received any indications since I had been shown my soul's ultimate purpose 30 years before. It was not that God had recognized me as His servant — that was still a long way away — but that it seemed God had now acknowledged my quest. In other words, this experience signified at the very least, that God accepted me as one of the candidates to be His servant.

Again, unexpectedly, the final latihan after the closing ceremony also granted me a similar experience; but this time, it was not God but Bapak's presence that I felt. Bapak was in the hall and from far above was looking down on us doing latihan, and I clearly felt that he was looking after me. Again, the feeling continued from the start to the end of the latihan.

That was the first time since Bapak's death that I had felt his presence. Both these experiences confirmed for me that the path I had chosen to walk up till then had not been wrong or mistaken.

Bapak described the normal soul as a small entity, like a dot, that is asleep deep inside us. That soul has buried within it a fragment of the Divine. When a person is 'opened' in Subud, the vast, universe-enveloping Power of God (which Bapak also called the Great Life Force) comes into contact with that fragment, causing a connection between the internal and external Power of

God so that the person's soul is then awakened. By maintaining that connection, the newly awakened soul grows and expands until it penetrates all parts of the body. It is only then that a person can become a fully functioning, complete human being, continuing on after death, transcending the earth and even the solar system, in order to return to the world that is the true world for human souls. This is the ultimate potential that the spiritual training of Subud offers to human beings.

However, to reach this point normally requires a lengthy process of purification and preparation; namely, the journey that is specific to each person's soul. Spiritual experiences act like signposts on the soul's journey, and are granted by God when necessary and when the time is right. But what one needs to be aware of is that there is a difference between the spiritual experience itself and living the content of that experience. Spiritual experiences are like having a thick curtain lifted and being given just a partial glimpse of the hidden spiritual world. These are like road signs or directions for us; but to actually live the truth that is revealed to us will require walking even further down a long road. On the other hand, we should also remember that there are people who have not even had one spiritual experience, yet in reality, such people are already 'living' these truths.

In other words, spiritual experiences are not necessarily a sign of spiritual advancement.

At the risk of repeating myself, I will also say that the contact with God's Power is not exclusive to Subud. When he visited

SUBUD – A SPIRITUAL JOURNEY

Europe for the first time, Bapak answered one of the members' questions in this way:

"God is the One who has the power, so that God also gives to whoever is able to receive it. So besides those in Subud, it is possible that many others can also receive. Therefore, it is not only in Subud, not only from Bapak. It [the Contact] already existed before Subud, for example in former times in the Christian religion, in the religion of Brahman or Buddha; in Islam it already existed. So it exists not only in Subud, but it may also be elsewhere. The only thing you need to know is the source, where it comes from, and this can be tested according to the ability that already exists within you."

Bapak then went on to say,

"And if you need to ask, Bapak has heard and knows that to find a contact with the power of God there are many methods that require an energy that is really difficult to imitate, or to follow, in other words through the way of reducing one's food, avoiding the pleasures of this world – in short by isolating oneself from society. Whereas in Subud, it is just the opposite; we should not abandon the needs and requirements of our life in this world." (Bapak's talks Vol.1–31; Code No.58 CSP 4)

Subud is not a path for the hermit or the recluse. Nor is it a path for 'special or selected people'. As mentioned before, Subud is an education and is a path for ordinary human beings to live their lives and experience inner growth. One of the features of

Subud is that it is compatible with both one's inner and outer life. The thoughts, emotions, and will that have no place in the latihan can be used instead to develop our outer lives to the full.

Finally, I will finish this book by describing my later life. I retired from international Subud duties in 1997 at the 10th Subud World Congress in Spokane, USA when I was 69. My final work had been as a Trustee of the Muhammad Subuh Foundation established in the USA to commemorate Bapak. The work of that Foundation was to promote the long-term development of Subud by providing financial support to poorer countries in order to build latihan halls, and to help the humanitarian, welfare and educational activities of Subud members all over the world.

After I returned to being a member of the local Japan group, I started two enterprises from zero with those who had worked with me in ISC, together with a younger member. It was in line with Bapak's wishes that Subud members should be able to stand on their own feet, inwardly as well as outwardly, and should be able to start enterprises both for themselves and for the benefit of other people. Our projects - one is commercial and the other is a non-profit organization, are still small but fortunately have gradually and steadily been developing. I am now preparing to hand them over to my successors. *(11th November 2005)*

EPILOGUE

In the second section of this book, I focused particularly on past spiritual experiences that had had a powerful impact on me. All of these experiences influenced the way I led my life and in some cases, were literally life-changing.

Besides those spiritual experiences, I was also given more external experiences and guidance on my journey, which were linked to my practical life. I omitted these from this book because it was difficult to prove whether the help from the power of God was behind these events, or whether they could be distinguished from the ordinary lucky/unlucky coincidences that anyone can have.

Made in the USA